Beautiful Hills of Home

Complete Poems of
Joseph Brickey

Copyright ©2011 & 2021 by Joseph Brickey
All Rights Reserved.
This book or any parts thereof
may not be reproduced by any means
without permission of the author.

First Edition

*To our first-born son, Joe Jr.,
who has gone home to be with
the Lord in heaven.*

About the Author

Joseph Brickey, Air Force Veteran, writer, amateur photographer, and avid hiker was born in Coeburn, Virginia on July 17, 1935. At an early age, he joined the US Air Force, and began a career that took him to remote and exotic places around the world including the Middle East, Far East, Africa and Europe.

Upon retirement from the Air Force, Mr. Brickey worked for General Dynamics and Lockheed-Martin in Fort Worth, Texas as a Technical Writer and Editor in verifying the quality and accuracy of technical publications for the F-16, F-111, A-12, and other Aircraft.

Mr. Brickey and his wife Shirley of almost 67 years are the proud parents of two sons, three daughters, and many grandchildren. He and his wife presently live in Tennessee.

Contents

Beautiful Hills of Home	2
A Beautiful New Day	3
A Beautiful River	4
A Beautiful Soul	5
A Beautiful World	6
A Gamble	7
A Good Man is Hard to Find	8
A Good Woman	9
A Letter to Our Son in Heaven	10
A Life That Matters	12
A Message of Love to Our Son	13
A Moment of Truth	14
A Mother's Prayer	14
A New American Blessing	15
A One Woman Man	16
A Peaceful Glen	17
A Restless Soul	18
A Rolling Stone	19
A Secret Place	20
A Silly Name	21
A Sinner's Prayer	22
A Soldier's Story	23
A Successful Life	24
A Time for all Things	25
A Wart on Her Nose	27
A Wedding Song, Gifts of Love	29
Along a Lonely Path	30
Always Be Kind	30
An Infant's Prayer	31
An Old American Blessing	32

An Old Man and His Dog	33
An Old Pickup Truck	35
Ancestors	36
Angels in Disguise	37
Autumn Dawn	37
Autumns of Yesterday	38
Beautiful Scenes	39
Beautiful Things	41
Before I say Goodbye	42
Before Time Slips Away	44
Born Again	45
Change	46
Character	47
Christ, The Hope of Mankind	48
Contradiction of Emotions	49
Cornbread and Buttermilk	49
Counting Blessings	50
COVID-19	51
Crossing the Fields to Home	53
Dare Devils	54
Days of Our Lives	55
Death of a Tree	56
Death Trap	57
Delay at Heaven's Gate	58
Do You See the Rose	58
Don't Forget to Pray	59
Don't go down that Road	60
Down a Country Road	61
Dreaming	62
Dreams	63
Encouragement	64
Faces	64

Faith Like a Mountain 65
Favorite Things..66
Final Goodbye..68
Forty Years Ago 69
Four-Leaf Clover..70
Ghosts of Vietnam 71
Give Me a Star..72
God, Family and Friends 73
God, Life, and the Universe...74
God's Gift of Trees 74
Have You Ever Wondered 75
He Loved This Land 76
Heaven 77
How Can We Measure the Cost..78
I'll Remember 79
I'm Sorry 80
If I Could Change the World 81
If I Could Read Your Mind...82
If I Could See Tomorrow...83
In An Instant..84
In Every Heart 85
Just a Boy Again 86
Just A Stranger 88
Just Trying to Get By...89
Kids 91
Let Us be Thankful 92
Let Your Conscience be Your Guide..92
Life's Record 93
Lonely, Lonesome Feeling...95
Lord, Let Me Go Easy 97
Lord, Count Me Down Slow 98
Lord, Turn America Around 99

Lord, We are Only Human	101
Lost Inspiration	102
Lost Moments	102
Love makes Everything Right	103
Man and Trees	104
Marriage	105
Memories Across the Years	106
Midnight Memories	107
Morning and Night	107
My Final Journey	108
My Heaven	110
My Prayer	111
New Shoes of Yesterday	113
No! It's Impossible!	114
Oh, I Must Go Back	115
Oh, So Long Ago	116
Oh, Glorious Morning	116
Paths of Life	117
Peace Like a River Flowing	118
Peace	119
People are Funny That Way	120
Pictures in My Mind	123
Precious Things	124
Reflections on Age and Time	125
Road Along the River	126
Safe at Home	127
Shadow on a Wall	127
Shirley Darling	128
Sleep	129
Someday	130
Somethings/Sometimes	131
Springtime	133

Stars in the Night	134
Take it Slow	135
Take it with a Smile	136
Tell Me You Love Me	137
Terms of Endearment	138
Texas Rain	139
TGIF	140
The Book of Life	141
The Case for Man	141
The Coal Miner	142
The Common Touch	144
The Destiny of Man	144
The Face in The Mirror	145
The Farmer	146
The Happy Hiker	148
The Happy Hunter	149
The Hiker's Prayer	150
The Joy of Children	151
The Life of a Man	152
The Little Church in the Valley	153
The Mountain of Life	155
The Old Country Store	156
The Old Home Place	157
The Old House	158
The Old Man's Poem of Secrets	159
The Old Mill by the Stream	161
The Old Oak Tree	162
The Optimist	163
The Pain of Regret	164
The Prodigal Son	165
The River of Time	166
The Wanderer	167

The Winter of 2015	168
Things I like About the West	169
Thinking Young	172
Thorns	173
Three Score Years and Ten	174
Tick-Tock, Tick-Tock	175
Time	176
To Really Live	176
Tree Swallows	177
True Friends	178
Two Roads	179
Valley of the Lonesome Pine	180
Walk with Me, Lord	181
Wanderlust	182
Waterfalls	183
What Are You	184
Wisdom of Years	185
Woman	186
Words	187
World of Death and Sorrow	188
You've Got to Laugh	189

Introduction

    This book is a composition of 95 poems from my first book and 86 poems published here for the first time in book format. All the poems are written using words and phrases easily understood by the man on the street.

It is my hope that the poems in this book will make you happy, make you sad, make you laugh, make you cry, help you understand God, life, death, time, the future, the past; rekindle childhood memories of home, family, love ones lost and appreciate love ones still living; that they will reveal the beauties of Nature as you take an imaginary hike along a wild mountain stream, walk beside a beautiful calm river, hike up a majestic mountain and across a lush green valley, down the river of life and up the mountain of life and give you a glimpse of the earth and stars as God placed them out in space; that they will return you to the hills of home and the old home place where you grew up; revive memories of family gatherings and the warmth and beauty of a family that are bound by their love for each other.

    These poems are also about romance, love and marriage, love lost and love won, true love and betrayal, young love and beautiful memories of a man and woman who have spent a life-time together. You will also find a poem about the love for and joy of children but another about the tragedy of a child gone astray.

    May the poems make you wonder about the mysteries of life: Why are we here? Where does our soul go when we die? Where is God and heaven? Is there life on other worlds? The question of the original sin and God's plan of redemption?

    May they also strengthen your faith in God, your love of family and friends and provide inspiration to always be your best and follow those principles that make us all better individuals. May they let you realize more clearly the brevity of life, but at the same time affirm again the hope we all have of eternal life by accepting Christ.

We have a saying in the mountains of SW Virginia that "You can take the boy out of the mountains, but you cannot take the mountains out of the boy." And I for one can speak to the truth of it.

The alluring beauty of the mountains, the forest, the rivers and streams, the majesty of the waterfalls, and the friendly and accommodating spirit of the people all act to entice one back home to the mountains. And let us not forget the beautiful women of English-Welsh, Scott-Irish, and Northern European decent whose ancestors settled in these mountains upon their arrival from Europe. Then add to the lovely beauty of the women the "soft as a falling-leaf accent of the southern mountains", and their sweet way of addressing everyone as "Honey, Darling, or Sweetheart", then one cannot help but be captivated forever and never wish to leave the mountains.

The men of these mountains also deserve mention because nowhere will one find more patriotic, dedicated, or loyal men to this great nation than in the Southern Appalachian Mountains. From the war for our independence to WW I and II, Korea, Vietnam, and the Mid-East Wars, they have served with distinction and valor, and many have given their lives for our freedom from the evils of socialism, communism and other totalitarian regimes of the world. That tradition of patriotism, loyalty and sacrifice continues today as many of their sons and daughters serve in our military.

Beautiful Hills of Home

It's for the Hills of Home I'm longing,
Back where the winds are blowing free,
And where the streams are flowing
Through meadows lush and green.

It's where a man can dream,
And make his dreams come true.
A place to find life's deepest meaning,
And start one's live anew.

It's where my loved ones are waiting
That I left so long ago.
How much I've longed to see them,
No one can ever know.

As a boy, I roamed those hills
So innocent and free.
With eagerness and wonder,
I waded every creek
And climbed every tree.

Now, the world has been my playground,
And many lovely places I have known,
But it is back to the hills I'm going
Where I always feel at home.

There's a rainbow over the hills,
And the fable I've heard is true:
There's a treasure at the end of the rainbow,
And that treasure, My Darling, is you.

A Beautiful New Day

The sun climbs up a bright blue sky,
And caresses the earth with its golden rays.
The earth still turns, the sun still shines,
All is well on a beautiful new day.

The storm of the night has passed,
And the air is clean and bright.
The birds are all singing in chorus--
A song of welcome to the morning light.

The flowers and trees are heavy with raindrops,
And tiny rainbows are bending the light.
The Dogwoods, Redbuds and Lilacs are in full bloom,
Could there be a more beautiful sight?

As I gaze in wonder at this scene of beauty and light,
The cares of the world seem far away.
And like the darkness of night,
My worries and cares have all taken flight.

And a prayer whispered softly comes to mind:
"Thank you Lord for a beautiful new day,
And may the beauty of this day fill all of our hearts--
Until all thoughts of anger and hate fade away."

A Beautiful River

There's a Beautiful River flowing
Through the memories of my mind,
And it's there my thoughts keep going
Back to a happier time.

In those long-ago days of my childhood
When the world was so new and bright,
My Dad, my brothers and I
Would hike to the river
To camp and spend the night.

I remember so well the swimming,
And how we would never tire.
And the fishing was fun,
And the fish tasted so good
When cooked over an open fire.

Around the campfire at night,
Dad would tell stories of the pioneer days of old--
Of how they braved the wilderness,
Indian raids, wild animals, disease and cold.
We kids would lie awake for hours
After the scary tales were told;
There could still be wild animals around,
And savage Indians could still be bold.

Now, many decades have passed,
And the years have taken their toll--
Dad and four brothers have passed away,
And I have passed from young to old.

But at night when the wind is blowing
In the pines at the top of the hill,
I can imagine the campfire glowing,
And I can hear their laughter still.

And in my memory,
The Beautiful River is still flowing,
And we are camping 'neath a starlit sky...
Those sounds and scenes are in
My thoughts and dreams--
And will be there till I die...

Most, if not all of us have met people who we know immediately are special because they display special qualities of having a beautiful soul.

These qualities include, but not limited to the following: kindness, compassion, mercy, love, forgiveness, generosity, etc., etc. They display no guile, greed, or envy to name a few negative traits. Not that they are perfect because none of us are, but they do display virtues much more than the average person.

A Beautiful Soul

Don't sell yourself short;
You are worth much more that you know.
Because worth is more than outward appearance,
It is really a matter of soul.

Because the soul is a reflection of our worth
And the beauty that dwells within--
Whether it be beautiful as a sunrise
Or whether it be ugly as sin.

One may be successful and famous
With wealth and money to spend,
But without a kind and generous spirit,
What are you really worth, my friend?

So, let us strive each day to discover
The beauty that dwells in our souls,
And suppress the evil that may lurk there---
Because a beautiful soul is worth more
Than all of earth's diamonds and gold.

My children, I give you one word of advice
When seeking a mate to share your life,
Don't marry for looks, position or gold,
But marry a person with a beautiful soul.

When at last my journey is finished
And my body is lying there lifeless and cold,
The words I hope will be said by all:
"He had a beautiful soul."

A Beautiful World

I'd like to take a space ship
To a distant star,
And look back on the earth
To see its beauty from afar.

Then I wouldn't see the conflicts
That divide the human race.
I'd see no hate and envy,
And the scenes of pain and hunger,
I wouldn't have to face.

I would see no death and suffering,
And the ravages of war and destruction
Would vanish without a trace.
I would see only earth's celestial beauty
As it shines there out in space.

God created the earth
As a perfect home for man.
Why can't we get alone?
Why can't we understand?
We're all God's children,
Brothers and sisters in His sight.
If we'd only love each other,
There'd be no cause to fight.

I doubt there is another world
In all the universe
As beautiful and as perfect
As the planet earth.
A paradise and garden for the human race,
A rare jewel of matchless beauty,
God suspended out in space.

A Gamble

How blessed is the man
Who finds a wife
That gives him love and affection
The rest of his life.

A wife that is honest, faithful and true
That never allows anything or anyone
To change her love for you.
Down through the years
Of struggle, hardship and care,
She's always beside you
The burdens to share.

In her eyes,
You'll always be her man,
Through the trials of life,
It's with you she'll stand.

But cursed is the man
Who marries a wife
That gives him nothing but trouble
The rest of his life.

He receives no affection,
And the relationship turns cold--
A mockery of the vows they took long ago.

Look upon this man
And pity him if you must,
But remember, marriage is a gamble
Built on love and trust--
For some that's a win,
But for many it's a bust
Because love can fade as well as trust.

A Good Man is Hard to Find

Come and listen all you young Ladies,
And I'll tell you a sad fact of our time--
When looking for a husband,
You can search the whole world over,
But a good man is hard to find.

Don't misunderstand me,
There is no shortage of men;
They are out there of every stripe and kind,
But few will measure up--
Because a good man is hard to find.

Now, this is not to say
No good men can be found.
There are a few out there somewhere,
But you will have to look around.

Always be wary of smooth talkers;
They'll fool you every time.
They are looking for fun and pleasure,
And marriage is never on their mind.

Some men will promise you the world
And luxuries of every kind.
But if you mention marriage,
They will desert you every time.

But never give up or be discouraged,
You will find your special man;
It is just a matter of time.
And in the end, it will all be worth it--
Because a good man is hard to find.

So, keep searching for a good man--
One that will be responsible, faithful and true.
He'll love, respect and stand with you--
No matter what others may do...

A Good Woman

(First Verse and Chorus)
If you got a good woman
  Who loves you,
If you got a good woman
  Who cares,
If you got a good woman
  Who adores you,
You are richer than a millionaire.

A good woman will always stand by you;
  She'll be there until the end.
She'll never leave or forsake you;
  She'll be your lover and friend.

She'll have your little babies--
  So beautiful and so fine.
She'll love you and the babies--
  Until the end of time.

She'll bake you cornbread and biscuits;
She'll cook you chicken and dumplings too.
  There'll always be love and affection,
  And to you she will always be true.

So treasure your woman always,
  And treat her with loving care.
'Cause if you got a good woman who loves you,
  You are richer than a millionaire.

Joe Jr., our first-born son, is now with the Lord in Heaven.

A Letter to Our Son in Heaven

My Dearest Son,
If only our tears could build a stairway to heaven,
And our love could bridge death's river wide,
We could cross the river and climb the stairs
To be forever by your side.

The Doctors tried so hard to save you,
And to God, Oh, how we prayed.
Now, our lives have no meaning...
Without your presence here each day.

How happy we were when you were born--
You brought so much joy and love.
You were our first-born child--
God's loving gift from heaven above.

To see your face would heal our broken hearts;
To hear your voice would dry our tears.
To hold you in ours arms again...
Would banish all the lonely years.

Oh, how much we miss you—
So lonely the days and nights.
Sweet memories of your life with us
Light up the windows of our hearts
And make the scenes so bright.

When will this pain and heartache end;
When will the tears stop forming?
Only when to heaven we go--
To join you there some joyous morning.

PS:
My Dearest Son,
You have joined the angels;
God has set your Spirit free.
You have made the great transition
From mortal man to life eternally.

Now, Enjoy the blessings of heaven,
And soon we will join you on that shore.
Then our family circle will be complete again--
To be broken nevermore.

A Life That Matters

A shooting star across the sky,
A flash of light and then it's gone.
That's our life span on the scale of time,
So brief, like the final words of a song.

Just a shadow on the wall,
Just a glimmer of light in the hall,
That's how quickly our lives are over;
It seems we hardly live at all.

So, If we would live a life that matters,
In the short time that God allows,
There's some things that we must do,
And we need to do them now.

First, seek the Lord and His Salvation
And live a life that's good and true.
Then, you'll be prepared for life eternal…
When this short life on earth is through.

Then, each day,
Let your words reach out in kindness
to the souls that live in doubt.
And let your actions be to lend a hand,
To lift them up and help them out.

Follow Christ in all His teachings,
"Do unto others as you would have them do to you."
Never disparage or judge friends and love ones,
Until you've walked a mile in their shoes.

Parents, Be kind and loving to you children,
And treat them with tender love and care.
And children,
Always honor and respect your Mom and Dad
Even when they seem unfair.

Be fair and honest in your dealings,
And never deceive, cheat or lie.
Because your reputation is your greatest asset,
And something money can never buy.

Always be generous in your giving,
And never stoop to cupidity and greed.
If God has blessed you with abundance,
Don't forget the folks in need.

Remember your life can be a blessing,
That can spark a mighty flame,
That will light this world of darkness,
Until the Lord comes back again.

A Message of Love to Our Son

Son, They tried so hard to save you,
But the Lord was calling you home.
Your body was weak and weary,
And God wanted you near His throne.

You are now with friends and loved ones
Who I know have welcomed you home.
Some day we all will join you--
To be part of God's heavenly throng.

You were our precious first born--
Such love and joy we gained.
Now we live in faith and hope--
Knowing we will be with you again.

As you walk beside the shinning river
With the Lord and loved ones gone before,
Remember, we love you and miss you so much--
You are in our hearts forevermore...

A Moment of Truth

As I stand here on the mountain,
And overlook the valley below...
A beautiful rainbow arches above me,
And peace and calm fill my soul.

Then suddenly all around me,
A great thunder storm is forming:
Rain and wind slashes; lightning flashes,
And across the valley, thunder rolls!

In that moment,
The truth of God's power to me unfolds:
No matter how chaos this world may be,
And though evil men may think they rule,
This is God's world; He is in control!

A Mother's Prayer

There's a light in a window for a child gone astray.
Placed there with loving hands by a worried Mother,
Who with an aching heart continues to pray
That her Darling Child will return home someday.

She walks the floor every night,
Tormented by thoughts of her lost child
And wonders if he's alright.
Every negative thought that one can imagine
Runs through her mind...
Is my child safe tonight, warm and secure
Out of the rain and snow?
Is he hungry, lost weight or become ill
From the wind and the cold?
Is he in good company,
Or has he taken up with a bad croud,
And now in jail is where he'll be found?
Will I ever see his dear face,
Or hear his laughter again?
In the throe of dispair, she pleads, "Dear Lord,
Let this nightmare end!"

As a baby, she held him close to her heart,
Always protective, nurturing and loving
To give him a good start.
Her greatest desire was for him to be happy
And to have a good life.
To be a man of honor and character,
To someday marry, have children and a loving wife.

But in spite of her love, guidance and care,
She now knows her worst fear.
Her son has lost his way,
And now wanders alone in the world,
she knows not where.

But a Mother's love will never allow her to give up or to fail.
Her prayers will still be pleaded from twilight till dawn,
And the light in her window will always be there---
Even when all hope is gone.

A New American Blessing

May your road of life be paved with gold, silver,
stocks and bonds,
And may you and your wife drive down
the road in a Ferrari and your kids in BMWs.
May you live in a mansion in a gated-community
And may your mortgage and debts be no more
than a couple million.

May you be the CEO of your own company
with an income of 7 plus-figures.
And may you employ many illegal aliens
for which you need not provide healthcare
or retirement benefits.

May your wife be the most beautiful woman in town,
President of her own company and never have an affair.
May your children test in the genius-level,
And win scholarships to the most prestigious schools
Where they study to become Doctors and Lawyers.

May your credit rating be above 800,
Your golf score below 70, your bowling score near 300.
May your second home be on the beach,
And if destroyed by a hurricane,
Uncle Sam replaces it as often as necessary.

May your CPA shield your income from the IRS
to reduce your taxes to zero,
And may the bulk of your wealth be in offshore banks
where it is hidden from the IRS.

May you live to at least 100
And never experience a divorce
due to your extramarital affairs.
May your kids never be involved in drugs
Or you wife with other men,
And may the death tax be repealed before you die.

A One Woman Man

I'm handsome and witty, or so I've been told,
And women love me because I'm charming and bold.
Once I had girlfriends all over the land,
But one look in your eyes and I'm a one woman man.

Chorus: I'm a one woman man, a one woman man.
A lot of hearts will be broken, but they must understand,
When a man loves a woman, he's a one woman man.

Was it your beautiful smile or beguiling eyes
That made me stop and realize:
My wild days are over and I understand--
When a man loves a woman,
He's a one woman Man.

I spoke to her Daddy, and he gave me her hand,
But he made me swear to be a one woman man.
I swore on the Bible as I raised my right hand
That I'd always be a one woman man.

Now, I'm happily married to my Darling wife,
To her I pledged my love for the rest of my life.
Then I kissed her sweet lips as I took her hand,
And now I'm forever a one woman man.

A Peaceful Glen

I'd like to be a great oak tree
Standing tall in a peaceful glen.
I'd sink my roots in the deep, dark earth--
Far away from the strife of men.

I'd lift my branches to the heavens above
And thank the Lord for his care and love.
Then bow my limbs down to the ground
And thank Him for the peace I've found.

I'd welcome kids to come and play--
To climb my branches as they sway.
Maybe have a picnic in my shade
And romp and play in the grassy glade.

Squirrels could climb my gnarly trunk
And flip their tails as they jump,
Then grab an acorn on the fly
And doze in the sun as the day goes by...

Birds could build their nests
And raise their young.
I would welcome all;
It would be great fun.
Deer and bear could wonder by
To feast on my acorns,
And get fat and spry.

The sun and rain would bless my days
As I grow strong and tall and hope and pray...
There'd be no war, no hate or crime,
But peace would reign for all time--
As the years go by in my peaceful glen--
Far away from the strife of men...

A Restless Soul

Some people are born with a restless soul,
And contentment may never be theirs to claim.
They'll search and strive to reach their goal,
And endure whatever the pain.

Some search for peace in service to God
Or in helping their fellowman.
To others, it is the beauty of Nature,
And in knowing that God created
The mountains, the rivers, and land.

Others may be driven by desire for adventure,
To find a lost city, new river or star.
But their restless spirit will not be content
Even when they find what they're looking for.

Now, A General may command an army
And fight for country, power and acclaim.
But will his mind be free of the horrors of war
When peace is restored again?

Many may strive for wealth and luxuries
With a mansion or a castle in Spain.
But I am just a simple man
With ambitions more, modest and plain.
Just give me a home, my wife and children,
And I will never complain.

Prestige and honor are some people's goal
With recognition, applause, and fame.
But just let me live free to do as I please
With a mind that is calm and sane.

To the restless souls, I must concede;
Their lives will never be dull or boring.
Some may travel the whole world over;
Their searching may never cease.
And if they find their fame and glory,
They may realize it all means nothing...
Until with God they have made their peace.

A Rolling Stone

I wish that I could find a place
Where I could feel at home.
I've wondered around the world so long,
I feel like a rolling stone.

A rolling stone gathers no moss--
No children, no wife, no home.
A rolling stone is ever lonely;
It rolls all alone.
I'd like to find a loving wife
And have children of our own.
We'd settle down in a little town
Where I could feel at home.

The neighbors would all be friendly--
They would smile and say, "Hello!"
The wife and kids would be my pride and joy,
And I never again would roam.

The kids would all be lovely
And always respectful and nice.
I'd take them hiking and camping;
We would have a wonderful life.

So, if you happen to know a lovely lady,
Who would like to be a loving wife
With children of her own,
Please let her know I'm ever ready--
To devote to her my life
And share with her a happy home.

A Secret Place

I'd like to find a secret place
That only God has seen.
A place of serenity and perfect peace
Where one could rest and dream.

A place of meadows, lakes and forests
And waterfalls in the stream--
And a rainbow arching above it all
To frame a perfect scene...

Where flowers and trees would ever bloom,
And time would seem to stand still.
And Spring would be forever---
With never a frost or wintry chill.

No graffiti would deface Nature's beauty,
Or trash and garbage pollute the streams.
And gaudy man-made structures
Would not spoil the beautiful scene.

Traffic noise would be unknown;
No smog or smoke would fill the air.
The stars would shine like beacon lights
Through night skies clear and fair.

No predator would prowl the tranquil nights---
Seeking innocent and helpless prey.
But violence would be forever banned,
And kindness would rule the day.

Is there such a secret place?
It is really hard to say.
Maybe in some remote corner of the world--
In a country far away...
Or maybe it will always remain a dream--
Because there may be no perfect place
On this earthly scene...

A Silly Name

A flash of gold, red and blue
Marked its path as it flew
And landed on a peach tree bloom
That blossomed in the month of June.

What creature can this be
So royally dressed festively
That effortlessly flies on a gentle breeze
And displays such beauty for all to see?

Could it be a fairy elf that no one has seen,
That God created while in a dream,
To brighten up this dreary world of pain
And give us all glimpse of heavenly things?

Butterfly, A silly name,
But who gave it the name, no one knows.
Despite all efforts, the mystery remains,
And may never be disclosed...

A Sinner's Prayer

Lord,
I come to you now, lost and alone.
I am tired and so weary,
I long to come home.
Although I am unworthy,
Please, from sin set me free.
Fill my heart with your love.
Let me walk close to thee.

Please grant me salvation,
From sin cleanse my soul.
Claim me as your own, Lord;
Take me into your fold.

Then, Please walk beside me--
Always near when I call.
Strengthen my faith, Lord--
Less from your grace I fall.

Give me a song, Lord,
Of worship and praise.
Let me sing of your love--
All of my days.

A Soldier's Story

On a high and lonely hill,
A marble stone marks the grave
Of a soldier true and brave,
Who for his Country gave
Blood, sweat and pain,
In a long-forgotten war,
That was known for blood and gore.

Sent by Uncle Sam
To the jungles of Vietnam,
To fight a war no one could understand.
There on a bare and bloody hill,
Where men were wounded
And men were killed,
The young soldier stood brave and tall,
And he almost gave his all
For that bloody piece of ground.

Bullets were cutting men down like a scythe;
More men were dead than were alive!
Mortars and grenades were exploding all around,
As brave men lay dead and dying on the ground!

Out-numbered ten to one,
And about to be overrun,
An urgent call brought Air Force planes,
That rained fire, steel and flame,
And the enemy was slain!
Had the jets not arrived in time,
Not a soldier alive would have been found
On that bloody battleground.

A Purple Heart and Star of Bronze could not suffice
For wounds that almost took the soldier's life,
And could never heal his mind
Of the anguish and the strife.

As he lay there in a hospital bed,
Filled with sorrow and with dread,
He relived the battle scene
That haunted his mind and his dreams.
Thoughts of young soldiers cold and dead
And the awful battle gore,
Would plague his thoughts for evermore.

Many years later, the soldier finally found sweet rest.
After much suffering, pain and death,
God has welcomed him to that peaceful shore…
Where there is no pain or war.

Dedicated to Spec 4 Bobby A. Hylton, US Army,
A True American Hero

A Successful Life

If I had my life to live over,
And could have a second chance,
I would get a better education
To ensure I could advance.

I'd study hard in school
And apply myself in every way.
One only goes through this life once,
So why not make it pay?

Why waste one's time on trivial matters,
That in the long run don't mean a thing?
Why not study to be a Doctor or Engineer
And really challenge your brain?

Some would say,
"I am too materialistic and only interested
in cold hard cash." To them, I would say,
"Without cash one can never support a family,
Help the less fortunate or achieve
the things that last."

So, young people,
Apply yourself boldly to everything you try,
But don't forget the other things that matter
That money can never buy.

Always be faithful to God, family, and friends
And live a life that is good and true.
Then you will be prepared for life eternal
When this short life on earth is through...

A Time for all Things

To everything, there is a season,
and a time to every purpose
under the heaven. Eccl. 3:1

A time to love
A time to hate
A time to give
A time to take

A time to live
A time to die
A time to laugh
A time to cry

A time to rejoice
A time to mourn
A time to praise
A time to scorn

A time for night
A time for day
A time to kneel
A time to pray

A time to drink
A time to eat
A time to awake
A time to sleep

A time to feel
A time to see
A time to stand
A time to flee

A time of war
A time of peace
A time to fight
A time to cease.

A time to lose
A time to gain
A time of infamy
A time of fame

A time of sun
A time of rain
A time to heal
A time of pain

A time to walk
A time to run
A time for work
A time for fun

A time to sew
A time to reap
A time for silence
A time to speak

A time to win
A time to lose
A time to doubt
A time to choose

A time to remember
A time to forget
A time to rejoice
A time to regret

A time to approve
A time to condemn
A time to borrow
A time to lend

A time to accept
A time to reject
A time to doubt
A time to expect

A time for speed
A time to slow
A time to stay
A time to go

A Wart on Her Nose

Julie was the subject of laughter,
ridicule and spite
As the kids at school all shouted:
"There's a wart on your nose!"
"There's a wart on your nose!"
But for Jim, It was love at first sight.
He saw the beauty of her soul.

So, Julie and Jim were Sweethearts
And planned to get married someday.
But then one morning, Julie awakened
To find that the wart had faded away!

She looked in the mirror, and to her delight,
Saw a face of youth, beauty, and grace.
At school that day, the kids didn't laugh,
But looked in amazement at Julie's
beautiful new face.

John, The most handsome boy in school,
Asked Julie for a date on Saturday night.
Julie, Flattered and elated said, "Yes!"
But she knew to hurt Jim was not right.
So, Julie and John became Sweethearts,
But Julie's conscience hurt her more every day.
And she noticed that John was selfish, unkind,
And shallow in every way.

Then one morning, Julie looked in horror
To see that the wart was back on her nose!
And the kids at school all shouted:
"There's a wart on your nose!"
"There's a wart on your nose!"
And handsome John, when he saw her,
Laughed and snidely walked away.

But when Jim saw Julie crying,
He took her in his arms,
Held her close and whispered,
"You're beautiful; I love you!"
And Julie sobbing, whispered, "I'm sorry;
I love you too!"

Postscript: Later, Jim and Julie were married.
They had three beautiful daughters,
But not one of them had a wart on her nose.

A Wedding Song, Gifts of Love

Groom Sings or Recites just before the wedding:

Close your eyes, My Darling; I have a gift for you--
A gift that will last forever as long as time endures.
I offer this gift to you alone;
It will always be just yours.

My gift to you is special, My Love;
Its value can never be told.
I hope you will treasure it always
As more precious than diamonds or gold.

The gift I offer, My Darling,
Is love with all my heart.
I ask you now to be my wife,
And pray we never shall part.

Bride Sings or Recites:

I accept your gift, My Darling,
With love so deep in my heart.
My gift to you will be just as true,
And I pray we never shall part.

My gift to you is also special.
Its value can never be told...
I hope you will treasure it always
As more precious than diamonds or gold.

Both Groom and Bride Sing or Recite Together:

Now, let us walk through life together
With love that is eternal and true.
May we always know the joy and happiness
That God has given to me and you.

Repeat the last verse if desired.

Along a Lonely Path

Along a lonely path,
Someday I'll meet my fate.
Will it be success and fortune,
Or failure, disgrace and hate?

Along a lonely path,
Someday opportunity may turn to gold,
And I will meet the Lord and Savior,
And He will renew my weary soul.

Along a lonely path,
Someday I'll find a home
With a loving wife and children
In a place to call our own.

Along a lonely path,
Someday this life will cease.
Then beside the shining river,
In the presence of God and family,
I'll find eternal peace...

Always Be Kind

There's a dear old Mother waiting alone,
Watching the clock and wishing you were home.
Give her a call and ease her mind;
She loves you dearly, so always be kind.

Dad has worked hard most of his life
To support his dear family and loving wife.
He's known hardship, illness and tragedy in his time;
He deserves your respect and above all be kind.

Grandpa and Grandma have been around for so long.
Don't take them for granted; God may soon call them home.
Make their last years joyful, peaceful and sublime;
Show them your love and affection and always be kind.

Good friends and neighbors are so hard to find,
And if you would keep them, always be kind.
Show kindness for kindness; it's easy to do,
They'll respect you forever and return kindness to you.

Our children and loved ones have the keys to our hearts,
And we'll love them forever whether they use them or not.
The keys are love, affection and kindness,
And we hope they'll use them a lot.

One can go through life being rude and unkind,
And go to one's grave with no peace of mind.
But showing kindness costs nothing, not even a dime,
And you will be remembered with kindness
If you show it in kind.

An Infant's Prayer

Oh, Mom, Let me live;
My life is in your hands
To take or to give.
Conceived in your womb,
A small infant am I,
Don't let them kill me!
Don't let me die!

Let me be born--a chance to live--
Your love to know, my love to give.
To feel your arms round me
And know that you care,
To grow up in the glow of your love so dear.

Let me know the wonder of living--
The joy and beauty of life,
And a Mother so precious
To love all my life.
Let me feel the rain, see the clouds and sky,
Hear the birds sing and watch them fly.
Let me run and play, let me laugh and cry.
Oh, Mom, Let me live! Don't let me die!

I am God's gift to you, don't throw me away.
Let me hear your voice as to God you pray.
Let me touch your face and see you smile.
Let me hear you call me your Darling Child.

Let me accomplish all I can
That God has planned for me...
What lives will I touch? What greatness achieve?
What joy will I give? What pain relieve?

The days and years their joy will declare--
So much happiness, warmth and love to share.
Family and friends will brighten my days.
Oh, Please let me live, Dear Mother, I pray.

But if you don't want me, then give me away
To a lonely couple who for a child they pray.
I'll give them my love, share their joy and fear,
And hope someday to know you, Mother...
Because I love you so Dear.

An Old American Blessing

May angels always fly above you,
And may God always bless and love you.
May happiness follow you like a rainbow after rain,
And may your spouse and children be your joy and fame.

May the road of life be smooth and ever sunny
with your pockets full of money.
May bread and meat be always on your table
and your health robust and able.

May your life be filled with treasure
of love from family, friends and neighbors,
And may you return to them full measure
all their kindness, love and favor.

May your life-span exceed 120,
And may you die before your spouse and children,
full of years, success and plenty.
And when you die,
may the Lord be there to meet you
with the words: "Well done", when He greets you.

An Old Man and His Dog

He was a frail little man who looked old and tired,
and his dog looked the same.
I saw them on the trail and as we drew near,
I mentioned that his dog was moving awfully slow.
The old man laughed and said,
"Yeah, I know; we are both getting old."

Then we struck up a conversation;
It seemed the natural thing to do.
We talked about the weather, politics,
our health and all the other common subjects
that most folks tend to do

From the old man's appearance,
I judged his age at 80 years or so,
but he told me he was 65,
and had had two heart attacks
which would make anyone look old.

Then, in a voice that expressed pride and compassion,
he told me about his dog--that he was 17 years old
and had been a good companion all those years,
but now like himself, had many health problems and
could barely walk and then only very slowly.

With a faraway look in his eyes,
the old man began to tell me about his life--
how he had been born in New Jersey,
but had lived in many cities around the Country.
I got the impression that his had been a lonely life
because he didn't mention a family,
and he didn't mention a wife

As the conversation ebbed,
We shook hands in parting,
and I felt I had made a friend.
"And by the way, what is your name?"
I asked. The old man replied,
"Oh, My name is Joe Flynn,
and this is my dog, Buster."

So, As you travel down the Trail of life,
you may pass an old man and his dog
that are moving kinda slow.
But don't ignore them or count them out;
they've traveled a lot of miles together,
and they still got a long way to go.

An Old Pickup Truck

An old pickup truck sits silent in a farmer's field,
Abandoned, neglected and rusting away.
Once the pride of the farmer and his family,
But now,
Only a place where spiders and mice go to play.

It once was beautiful, bright and new,
Prized by the farmer to haul
Corn, tobacco, potatoes and hay.
But now, useless like a worn-out tool,
Broken, abused and thrown away.

If caught in time,
It could have been restored like new.
But now, it's too late!
Rust and the elements have sealed its fate,
And time has taken its due.

Proudly,
The farmer once drove his family to church
And to town on Saturday to shop.
For thousands of miles,
The old pickup rolled down the road;
It seemed it would never stop.

But finally, like the farmer,
Age and miles took their toll.
The old farmer passed away and
Now rests in peace on top of the knoll.
And the old pickup
Sits motionless in the farmer's field,
Its engine forever--silent and still.

Ancestors

Far below in its bed of stone,
The silent river flows on its way.
High on the slopes of the ancient hills,
Our ancestors sleep in their beds of clay.

What turn of fate brought them to this lonely place?
What right or wrong made them love or hate?
Were they blessed with wisdom, courage and grace?
What were their dreams, their goals, their fate?

They braved a wilderness--remote, alone.
New lands they sought to build their homes.
To raise their families as they might,
And worship God in freedom's light.

With plow, ax, and gun, they tamed this land.
With courage and resolve, they made their stand.
Independent, resourceful, they could not fail.
With blood, sweat, and tears, they would prevail.

Their needs were simple and luxuries were few.
Their lives austere and motives true.
Men and women brave and bold,
They endured Indian raids, disease and cold.

To our ancestors, there's honor due.
Our Country is great because they were true--
To God, Country and families too.
They fought wars to keep us free,
And passed along to you and me
The greatest Country in history.

Angels in Disguise

Who treats us with sensitivity, dignity and loving care?
Who brings an aura of warmth and compassion to our room
By her presence there?
Who, by her kindness and encouragement,
Our spirits revive, and through her knowledge and skill,
Relieves our pain and helps us survive?
She is God's gift to mankind--a Nurse, an Angel in Disguise.

Who is always present during disaster and war
To treat the injured and wounded their health to restore?
Who braves the dangers of turmoil and disease
To releive the suffering of the poor and despised?
She is God's gift to the world--a Nurse, an Angel in Disguise.

Who is by our bed side when death hovers near
To relieve our pain and calm our fear?
Who changes despair to hope by her gentle style,
And brightens the darkest hours by the warmth of her smile?
She is God's gift to us all--a Nurse, an Angel in Disguise.

Autumn Dawn

There is a magic light in the morning
Like no other time of day
As the autumn sun awakens the earth
With its golden rays.

A cool breeze seems to whisper
That all is well and new...
As the sun chases shadows
Across a sky turning blue...

The rooster is awake and crowing;
The birds are singing too,
And rainbows by the millions
Are sparkling in the dew.

The mountain tops are glowing
With a golden sheen,
And grey fog is drifting down the valley
O're the meadows and the stream.

Hoarfrost is on the clover,
The flowers and the trees,
And sunbeams are dancing
On the grasses and the leaves.

A doe and her fawn are grazing
Underneath the apple trees,
And a mourning dove is cooing
A lonely melody.

Leaves everywhere are turning---
Gold, brown and red,
And geese in V-formation
Are cruising overhead.

Mom is calling to her kids:
"Wake up sleepy heads;
There's no more time for dreaming.
Your breakfast is waiting,
And then it's off to school.
Your Dad has already gone to work,
And I have things to do."

Autumns of Yesterday

Autumn leaves have turned;
The nights are cold and child.
Frost is on the ground;
The woods are silent and still.

Summer has come and gone;
The flowers have faded to gray.
We spent our time in the sun,
　Now winter is on its way.

The corn is in the crib;
The hay is cut and stacked.
Apple butter was boiled and canned;
Walnuts are hulled and cracked.

Apples were picked and stored;
Pumpkins and can stuff line the walls.
Geese are flying south;
We can hear their honking calls.

Beans were picked and dried;
Potatoes are in the bin.
The kids are back in school;
Vacation is at an end.

Feather beds are stuffed;
The quilts are clean and soft.
The kids will be warm and snug
Sleeping in the loft.

The smokehouse is filled with bacon;
Cabbage and turnips are in the berm.
There's coal and firewood in the shed,
So, we have no fear of winter--
Because there is plenty of food to eat
And plenty of fuel to burn...

Beautiful Scenes

Is there anything as beautiful as:
A Mother's kind and loving face
A baby girl dressed in bows and lace

Sunrise over a snow-capped peak
A baby's smile as it sleeps

Swallows in their graceful flight
Butterflies in the morning light

A rainbow after a summer rain
A Blue Bird outside the window pane

Sunrise and sunset gold
A deep blue lake framed by winter snow

Tiny rainbows in the morning dew
A loving wife that's always true

Fall foliage that has turned to red and gold
A barefoot boy with his fishing pole
An old man with a kind and gentle soul

A Clipper Ship in full sail
The ocean calm after a gale

Church bell chimes in the early dawn
A mother deer and her fawn

A bright red rose in full bloom
A blushing bride in early June

Mother and daughters in their Easter dress
A baby held to its Mother's breast

Lilacs blooming in early spring
Sweethearts strolling down a country lane

Rainbows in ocean spray and waterfalls
A Mourning Dove when it calls

A ballerina's poise and grace
A young daughter's kiss on her Daddy's face

I am sure there are many more than these.
Please feel free to visualize as many as you please.

Beautiful Things

A spring in the desert
A rainbow after a storm
A hug from our kids
Cry of a baby when it's born

Cool drink when we are thirsty
A fire when we're cold
Food when we're hungry
Kindness when we're old

A friend when we're lonely
Familiar trail when we're lost
A bed when we're sleepy
An anchor when we're tossed

A friendly face in the crowd
A smile when we're low
A prayer whispered softly
Peace in our soul

A butterfly on a bloom
A hummingbird in flight
Lonely wind in the pines
A train whistle in the night

Taste of honey on our tongue
Sound of music to our ears
Voices of long-lost loved ones
Whispered softly across the years

Our kids when they were young
A fish on the line
Mom and Dad waving from the porch
Sweet memories back in time
Watermelons on the vine
Apples on the tree
Picnic by the stream
Together, you and me

Roses in bloom
Swallows on the wing
First light of dawn
Birds when they sing

Wild river in the mountains
Peaceful lake on the plain
Never a sad goodbye
A world without pain

Peach blooms in April
Apple Blossoms in May
Joy at seeing loved ones
Peace when we pray

First kiss from my Sweetheart
A wedding in June
Question: "Do you take this woman?"
Answer: "I do."

A hike in the mountains
Waterfalls in the stream
A world without strife
Fulfillment of a dream

Before I say Goodbye

Lord, I know our days are numbered,
And the count is so quickly complete,
But before I say Goodbye,
Let me linger a little while
To enjoy this life so sweet.

Lord, Before I say Goodbye,
Let me linger a little while--
To see the innocence of my baby's smile
And know the joy of a loving wife
As we face together the trials of life.

Lord, Before I say Goodbye,
Let me linger a little while--
To see the glow on my Darling's face
As I kiss her lips and we embrace.
And let me know the warmth
of a loving home
Filled with children of our own.

Lord, Before I say Goodbye,
Let me linger a little while--
To know the love and kindness
of friends and family along the way...
As our lives are passing day by day.

Lord, Before I say Goodbye,
Let me linger a little while--
To feel the sunshine of early spring
And see the flowers bloom after a gentle rain.
Let me walk along a mountain stream
And know the peace that nature brings.

Lord, Before I say Goodbye,
Let me linger a little while--
To gaze in wonder at the starry sky
And watch the seasons change
as the years go by.
Let me see the beauty of dawn's
early light
As a new day breaks with the
passing night.

Lord, Before I say goodbye,
Let me linger a little while--
To see my children grow up and know success
And find peace, love and happiness.
Then, I'll be ready to say Goodbye with style,
And I'll thank you Lord for letting me
linger a little while.

Before Time Slips Away

Have you lived a life of sin and self-destruction?
From your Mother's teachings have you strayed?
God is waiting to heal your broken spirit—
Before time slips away...

Have you hurt your loved ones deeply
By unkind words that one should never say?
It's never too late to plead, "I'm sorry."—
Before time slips away...

Have you been betrayed by false friends,
Or by an unfaithful love along the way?
Don't let it make you bitter; start your life anew--
Before time slips away...

Do you feel your life has been a failure--
That you've achieved nothing worthwhile anyway?
Today, begin to live your dreams--
Before time slips away...

My Dear Children,
You have your lives before you,
And you're free to live them day by day.
But remember to be faithful
To God, friends and loved ones--
Before time slips away...

Born Again

I heard a call from heaven--
A longing in my soul.
I fell upon my knees
As the tear drops flowed.

I asked the Lord for mercy--
My sins to forgive;
To take away my shame,
For Him I longed to live.

Then a great joy came o'er me;
My heart and mind were free of sin.
The Lord had redeemed my weary soul!
I was born again!

Then the World looked so different--
So bright, so clean and new.
The trees and flowers looked so lovely
And the sky a brighter blue.

Through God's love,
I saw people in a beautiful light--
Oh! How their faces did glow!
I knew then we were all precious in His sight,
And He longed to redeem our sinful souls.

So, if you ever hear a call from God
That seems to say, "*My child come home.*"
I pray you'll answer the call at once
And let Christ your sins atone.

No greater life can one ever live
Than a life that is free from sin.
No greater joy can one ever know
Than when you are born again.

Change

Of all the things most certain,
Change seems to be the most sure.
Because few things stay the same,
And few things will endure.

As winter changes to Spring,
And Summer turns to Fall,
The cycle seems so constant
As the four seasons we recall.

Now, the universe seems forever;
It is always there for us to see.
But the sun and planets are in flux
As they move around with the galaxies.

Man, who is born of woman,
Is destined for a life of change.
As he matures in mind and body,
Nothing ever stays the same.

So, Is there anything on which we can rely
In this life of change and endeavor?
Yes, The answer of course is God!--
The same yesterday, today, and forever...

Sometimes we fail to realize that our character is on display every day by the words we speak and values we project when dealing with people. I personally believe that our character is a product of heredity and environment. But I also think that our negative values can be changed and positive ones adopted at any time we desire. It is up to the individual.

Character

It is said, "You are known by the company you keep,
By the words you use and how you speak,
But values define one's character as strong or weak."

Honesty and honor rank high on the list--
Can you be trusted, or is dealing with you a constant risk?

Are you unbiased and fair to all--both rich and poor,
Or does wealth and fame influence you more?

Responsibility and integrity are traits admired.
When things go wrong, do you avoid and deny,
Or boldly declare, "Mistakes were made, I will not lie."

Generosity marks a person with a loving soul
Who gives of his wealth and time--
The poor or aggrieved to console.

Loyalty and devotion stamps a person
Of principle who stands firm and strong.
They are by your side when things go wrong.
Courage and boldness is respected by all.
Without it, no war can be won,
And great kingdoms will fall.

Kindness and sympathy are the signs of a tender heart
That understands sorrow when loved ones depart.
Comfort and support is given when needed the most
By people of character without cost or boast.

These values mark one's character as strong or weak.
But we are free to choose what values we embrace
And what company we keep.

Christ, The Hope of Mankind

Is there anything new under the sun
Since man was created and time begun?
There has always been conflict.
There has always been strife.
It is all part of living;
It is all part of life.

Some things never change--
Get better or worse...
There is living and dying,
Marriage and birth,
And struggle for power by
Kings of the earth.
And evil still prevails;
It is a continuing curse.

Will man ever live in harmony and peace?
Will terror ever end? Will hate ever cease?
In the name of religion, some kill and maim,
As they call on their god,
But their prayers are in vain.

For 86 long years I have walked on this earth.
I have seen it all--the best and the worst.
The beautiful and ugly, the good and the bad.
The rich and poor, the happy and sad.

Now, as my years dwindle down,
To a few on this earth,
I often wonder what life is worth.
Man is born of woman into sorrow and pain,
Of strife and struggle, heartache and shame.
At death, his body is returned to the earth--alone,
And the soul departs for worlds unknown.

For man, is there life beyond the grave,
Or is all hope lost at the end of his days?
Thank God!, There's still hope in Christ, The Lord --
God has promised eternal life to all men
If they accept His Son and repent of their sin...

Contradiction of Emotions

The call of the Mourning Dove,
The whisper of wind in the Pines,
Or of a distant train whistle in the night
Awaken in us a contradiction of sadness
And pleasure and of bitter sweet memories.

Cornbread and Buttermilk

To exotic lands I've traveled,
And their food tastes mighty fine,
But it takes cornbread and buttermilk
To satisfy that hungry craving in my mind.

You can have your caviar, hors d'oeuvres
And finger food and eat every bite.
Just give me cornbread and buttermilk
To whit my appetite.

It's country food a body needs
To sustain it through the day,
When there's work to be done,
Like cutting alfalfa, wheat and hay.

My Mommy raised eleven kids;
They all grew up strong and healthy
And were thankful every day
For cornbread and buttermilk--
That tasted, "Oh, So good!",
And kept their hunger at bay.

Counting Blessings

If my life should cease tomorrow,
And my time on earth should end,
I still could not count all my blessings—
What a wonderful journey it has been.

When I see my Darling smiling,
Or hear my children laugh at play,
And my love ones gathered round me
As each night we kneel to pray--
Then I know the many blessings
That the Lord has conveyed,
And I am thankful for them all--
As I count them day by day.

When I awaken in the morning
To a bright and sunny day;
Or walk along a mountain stream
And see the flowers bloom in May;
Or view waterfalls and sunsets
That take my breath away--
Then I know the beauty of Nature
And feel blessed in every way.

Whcn I see old glory waving o'er
Our Country blessed and free;
And I hear the song of freedom
Ringing out from sea to sea,
Then I know the many blessing
That the Lord has given me,
And I pray He will be honored
As He used to be.

But sometimes life can be trying,
But the good outweighs the bad--
Could there be a greater blessing
Than a loving Mom and Dad?
And there's brothers and there's sisters,
And aunts and uncles too,
And all the other loving people
That make our dreams come true.

So, I will keep on counting blessing
Until my life on earth shall cease--
Then I'll meet you up in heaven
In that land of joy and peace.
There with our Lord and Savior
And our friends and love ones too,
We'll forever count our blessings--
Because all our dreams come true.

COVID-19

Out of China it came--The Dark Shadow of Death--
Spreading its wings over the earth on its evil quest!
Infecting millions, but killing mostly the old
As it raged like wildfire out of control!

President Trump rallied the Nation,
And his quick action saved thousands of lives!
With VP Mike Pence heading his team,
The Country was ready to battle COVID-19!

As the cases and death counts rose,
A Country lock down was imposed!
With no vaccine or cure,
The virus spread its chaos and fear!

Doctors and Nurses on the front line--
Quarantined from families long periods of time.
Testing and treating the sick and dying,
Showing incredible courage, there's no denying.

Isolation required of family and friends,
Gatherings allowed, but no more than ten.
Stay six feet apart to prevent its spread--
Drastic action to reduce the sick and dead.

Country in lock down, businesses closed,
Economic disaster could soon unfold.
Loans to small businesses approved,
And gifts of money for every citizen to use.

Hoarding and panic created by fear
Caused TP and food to be scarce and dear.
No traffic on roads even with gasoline cheap.
Price driven down by "stay at home rules"
That for our own safety we all must keep.

Airlines grounded with world traffic in decline,
But big trucks and trains running on time.
Across the Nation, our greatest lifeline--
Delivering food and supplies 24 hours a day,
How grateful we are and for their safety we pray.

Never in history has a virus so quickly spread.
Was it by accident or on purpose to create fear and dread?
Or was it an act of war in disguise
To destroy our economy and take our lives?
Or was it God's punishment to this world of sin
Who have rejected his laws and turned their backs on Him?

Memories:

Memories are wonderful, but can be painful, especially of loved ones and friends who have passed away. But to me there is a golden glow associated with those wonderful memories that gives me hope and comfort. The following poem is dedicated to all of my loved ones who have gone on to be with the Lord. They are often in my thoughts, dreams and memory.

Crossing the Fields to Home

How carefree those days when just a boy,
I roamed the fields of home.
From dawn to dust with old Jack, my dog,
Now memories are all I own.

Those memories cause the tears to flow
When I recall the family fold--
And the joy and love we shared back then
In that wonderful place so long ago...

Mom and Dad were always there;
They were our guiding light.
They raised us kids with love and care,
And taught us wrong from right.

Life could be hard back then;
There was always work to do.
In the heat of summer and cold of winter,
Early to bed and early to rise
Was the family rule.

Sometimes, there was pain and sorrow--
Little Janie took sick in the spring,
And we lost her when the swallows came.
It broke our hearts to hear her cry,
And when she pleaded,
"Mommy, I don't want to die."

Now, so many years have passed,
And it's nothing like back then we knew.
Somethings are better; somethings are worse---
Depending on one's point of view.

As the sun sinks low behind the lonely hills,
And I am sitting here all alone--
In my memory, I see the old home place
With Mom and Dad and all the kids,
And old Jack and I are crossing the fields to home...

Dare Devils

Some people live on the edge--
Between life and eternity.
They climb the highest mountains
And cross the raging seas.

They climb every waterfall
Though slick with mud and slime.
If they fall from the top,
Their lives ain't worth a dime.

They visit poison reptiles,
And take portraits in their dens.
Then charm them with sweet words
And call them buddies and friends.

They stand on the eagle's perch
And dance all around.
They leap between great boulders
With no fear of falling down.

They scale huge cliffs and boulders
And laugh all the while.
Fun and excitement is their forte,
And courting danger is their style.

Neither Rain, sleet or snow
Deters their eager spirit--
The weather they ignore.
The next adventure is their goal;
They are out to make a score

Some people think they are crazy
While others say,
"They are just young and spry."
But I'd say they are just folks like us,
But like to get their kicks--
By looking danger in the eye.

Days of Our Lives

The earth revolves around the sun
As the seasons come and go.
All life on earth is measured in time,
But when it ends, God only knows.

Man may live 80 years or so--
Before he passes away.
But how long we live matters less--
Than how we spend each day.

When you come to the end of your journey,
Will you look back on your life with pride,
And know you have done your best?
Or will you feel guilt and shame
Because you failed life's toughest tests?

Did you squander life's precious moments
On some vain and frivolous game,
Or was your life sincere and fruitful
With little thought of wealth or fame?

Were things left undone or words unspoken
That could have eased someone's pain?
If you had a second chance,
Would you live your life the same?

Time is short and life is fleeting;
Don't live your life in vain.
Set your goals and make your mark
On the score board of life's plain...

Death of a Tree

Once I was a mighty oak tree of beauty and grace
With hundreds of branches that vied for space.
On a great trunk over a hundred feet high,
My limbs reached toward heaven and God in the sky.

In summer, I was adorned in beautiful green leaves
That played a sweet melody as they caught every breeze.
In fall my leaves turned a golden brown,
And my friends in the forest dined on my acorns
That fell to the ground.

People admired my beauty as they passed by--
Awed by my girth and branches so high.
Favored by birds and squirrels to build their homes,
I welcomed their presence; I was never alone.

For centuries I stood in the forest regal and free.
Embracing Mother Earth, she nourished my life
From tiny acorn to a towering oak tree.
My roots drank deeply from the earth's rich store--
My expected lifespan was a thousand years or more.

But those wonderful years I was never to see!
A logger entered the forest and
Felled all my offspring, and then, he cut me!
Oh! The terrible pain as he cut off my limbs
And sawed through my trunk!

As I fell to the ground,
The logger laughed at my fate and shouted in triumph!
Where once there had been a mighty oak tree--
There is now only a stump!

The following poem is dedicated to those who have lost their lives while jumping from a waterfall or swimming in a pool below, and to their loved ones and friends who will never stop loving them, missing them or grieving for their loss. May the words of this poem also give pause to future young men and women who may be thinking of risking their lives in any way around waterfalls.

Death Trap

A magnificent waterfall gleaming in the sun,
Plunging from a cliff over 50 feet high--
A death trap, a magnet to young women and men
As they challenge death and leap from the rim.

Go ahead; make your jump now
If injury or death you would see!
A broken neck, paralyzes for life,
Or a crushed skull is yours for free!

Are you tempted to jump to a challenge or dare,
Or for bragging rights to friends at school?
Or to prove your courage, then please beware!
Is it really worth risking your life to do?

One slip, miscalculation, or awkward step
Could cut your jump short resulting in death.
As you strike the cliff or drown in the pool below,
There death will take your life and God your soul.

Around waterfalls, many young people have died.
If only they knew how their loved ones cried,
Or how great was their loss to family and friends,
Or that their broken hearts will never mend...

No price can be placed on your life so dear.
A gift from God, so precious, don't let it end here!
Walk away! Walk away now!
Don't give in to a foolish whim!
Your life is worth more, so much more
To you, your family and friends!

Delay at Heaven's Gate

If God will grant me the love of friends and family; and allow me to see the mountains ablaze with the blooms of Rhododendrons and Azaleas in June, and to feel the soft rain on a bright Spring morning, and to walk along a wild mountain stream and hear the thunder of a great waterfall up close, and to view a wide green valley with high blue mountains in the distance, and to hear the ocean surf and to taste and smell the salt mist as the waves break against seaside cliffs, and to see the smile on the lovely face of my Darling Wife and hear the laughter of our children as they walk by our side--then I won't mind at all if St Peter delays me at heaven's gate, and I hear him say, "Don't rush me, Joe; you have had more than your share of heaven on earth already."

Do You See the Rose

In the garden of life with its beauty and strife,
Do you see the beauty or only the misery and woe?
We can spend all our time, but we will never find
a perfect world here below.
Do you see the thorns, or do you see the rose?

There are flaws to be found if we look around.
No one is perfect we know.
But there is good in most men as well as some sin,
Do you see the thorns, or do you see the rose?

One can climb a high mountain peak
And look down on the world below.
There is misery down there,
Or there is happiness to share.
Do you see the thorns, or do you see the rose?

As we walk through this life,
We can look for the good as we all should
Or find fault wherever we go.
But what a shame it would be if we only see--
-Thorns-
And never the beautiful Rose.

Don't Forget to Pray

Sometimes our lives seem so hopeless,
So many misfortunes have come our way.
Lost jobs, separation and illness
Seem to plague us day after day.
But remember,
God can help us solve any problem,
Don't forget to pray.

Sometimes we reach the depths of depression.
We may have lost a friend or loved one,
And our hearts are breaking every day.
But God's love can help us bear the heartache,
Don't forget to pray.

Many loved ones are in the Service
Defending freedom every day.
Dear Lord, Please send your Guardian Angels
To protect them as they go in harm's way.
Bring them home safely to their families
To fight another day.

In this life, it seems there will always be misfortune,
And many problems are here to stay.
It seems all a part of living,
That we must endure along the way.
But our lives can be more peaceful,
And many problems will just fade away--
If we only trust the Lord and Don't Forget to Pray.

There are good roads and bad roads and some we should never take.
Some will lead to love and happiness and some to trouble and hate.

Don't go down that Road

Sometimes this life don't seem worth living.
There's heartache, pain, and sorrow everywhere---
Why must we bear such a heavy load?
But let it not discourage or defeat you;
Don't go down that road!

Are you on the road of self-destruction
From the sinful seeds you have sown?
If you would win the game of life;
Don't go down that road!

Has your love-life gone to pieces
And at work you've been let go?
Time will surely solve these problems.
So don't wallow in the self-pity mode;
Don't go down that road!

Have friends and neighbors turned against you
With vicious lies that friendships can corrode?
Don't let it drag you down to their level;
Don't go down that road!

Our Nation is in a state of chaos
From actions that deny God's moral codes.
Such a nation cannot long endure;
We can't go down that road!

There's a road that leads to heaven
And a beautiful heavenly abode.
It's a road to eternal life and happiness;
May we all go down that road!

Down a Country Road

In my memory,
There's a country road a'winding
Through a valley lush and green,
And it's there my heart is pining
For an old familiar scene.

The road crosses a meadow
To an old farm house among the trees,
And I'm just a lad again,
And my Mom is calling me.

On barefoot wings of youth,
I close the space between us,
And on her loving face I see
A welcome smile of gladness
As she looks at me.

In her eyes there's a kindness
That only a Mother can show,
And in her bosom beats a heart of love
That only God bestows.

Later, as a young man returning from the war,
I am walking down that country road to home,
and I see my family waiting at the gate.

Instantly, Mom's arms enfold me
As tears of joy stream down her face,
And it seemed that time stood still
In that wonderful time and place.

Then Dad and the other kids gathered 'round me,
And on their faces a love-light shown.
And Dad's gentle words of welcome
I'll always remember:
"Son, It's so good to have you home."

How I wish that I could return
To that time so long ago
When our family was all together,
And the pace was easy and slow.

We thought it would never end,
But time always takes a heavy toll--
Mom and Dad have long since passed away,
And the kids left home long ago.

So, now there are only memories,
But those memories have a golden glow
Of lives that were so warm and beautiful...
Down a Country Road...

Dreaming

I am a young Ground Hog
Sleeping peacefully in my den,
And dreaming about green fields of clover
When Spring Time is here again.

And I am dreaming about the pretty female
Living with her mother across the field.
And how I'd love to hear her melodious whistle
That sounds so sweet and shrill.

We will frolic in green fields of clover
When Spring Time rolls around.
And raid the old farmer's melon patch
That he has planted in new ground.

And soon I'll ask her to be my bride,
And hope she will say, "I will".
We will raise a family of our own,
Then there will be a chorus of whistles
From the fields and meadows--
That sound so sweet and shrill...

Dreams

How pleasant our sleep when we experience a dream
That takes us back to a childhood scene.
Or a dream that reminds us of a love we once knew,
Or of a family gathering and friends that were true.

How warm the feeling in a dream to see
The faces of loved ones, who have left the scene,
And to relive again the joy of their presence,
If only for a moment in a fleeting dream.

Dreams can lift our spirits or make us feel low,
Can take us to heaven or to hell down below.
They can inspire us to accomplish our goal,
Or drag us down and damage our soul.

Why do we dream of places and people
That we don't know?
Or have nightmares of demons and monsters
That make our blood run cold?
Is it something we ate,
Or fears that haunt us from long ago,
Or have the covers slipped off
And our feet are cold?

I remember a dream while still a young man,
Of a beautiful girl who was faithful and true.
And when I first saw your face, I knew--
The girl in my dream, My Darling was you!
I thank God that some dreams come true!

Encouragement

Life's road is so hard to travel,
And mistakes we all have made
Through unkind words or deeds.
But please,
let us not judge or condemn each other,
Encouragement to do better is what we need.

No one in this life is perfect.
If we were,
Forgiveness, there would be no need to plead.
But we must strive to be more Christ-like,
And encouragement is what we need.

It's so easy use bad judgement
In a moment of weakness or greed.
No one should condone our bad behavior,
But encouragement to mend our ways is what we need.

Christ gave his life to redeem you
From the sinful life you lead.
Accept him now and gain life eternal;
His words of encouragement are what you need.

Faces

On the street of life,
I see the faces of mankind.
The expressions they wear
Reflects their state of mind...

How could we ever forget the vision
Of innocence on the face of a child,
Or the laugh-lines carved by time
On an old man's face by his smile?

Have we all not seen the love in a Mother's eyes
As she gazes in wonder at her new-born child?
And have we not witnessed the sadness on faces
At the loss of a loved one
That brightened their lives for a while?

Or tears of joy on the faces of families--
United after years apart,
And the smiles that reflect the joy
In their hearts.

Can we ever imagine the thrill it will be
To see the face of Christ, our Savior
And God, the Father, on His throne.
There surrounded by loved ones,
Whose dear faces we'll see as eternity rolls on.

Faith Like a Mountain

By Faith,
I've climbed to the mountain top,
And now my troubles all look small.
They're so far down below me
I can hardly see them now at all.

I put my faith in the Lord,
And what a relief it has been.
I don't worry about tomorrow;
I am trusting now in Him.

This old world is full of trouble,
And sometimes my faith gets low.
But there is comfort on the mountain
Where God's cooling breezes blow.

Now, I am looking at the sunset
As the night shadows fall.
But I don't worry about the darkness
Because Christ is ever near me
And will always hear my call.

So, I'll stay here on the mountain
And keep my doubts and fears below.
Because the Lord is always with me
When to the mountain top I go.

Favorite Things

Misty rain in early Spring
A harvest moon that autumn brings

Waterfalls and mountain streams
Peaceful sleep and beautiful dreams

Picnics under great Oak Trees
A shady glen and a cooling breeze

Blue Birds and Swallows in their flight
The call of the whippoorwill on a summer night

Three lined streets in an old town
The fragrance of hay and new plowed ground

Hiking trails that lead to waterfalls
The sound of the Mourning Dove when it calls

Old houses that seem to say, "Come in."
A smile and handshake from my friends

Snow-capped peaks at first light of dawn
Music and words of a great old song

Biscuits baked to a golden crust
The magical glow at dawn and dust

Early spring when new life is born
A beautiful rainbow after a storm

Moon and stars on a crystal-clear night
My Darling's smile and eyes so bright

Old trucks and cars with running boards
Swinging bridges and river fords

Old bicycles painted red, white and blue
Friends and loved ones who are always true

My kids' wet kisses on my face
A Soldier returned from war sound and safe

Grandma and Grandpa with faces so kind
Good friends and neighbors--so hard to find

Memories of childhood so long ago
Mom and Dad and the family fold

Beautiful Roses in full bloom
Wedding bells in early June

A baby's smile as it sleeps
Tears of joy that a Mother weeps

Ghost towns of the early West
A Rocky Mountain with snow-capped crest

Old western movies and their heroes
Running horses and buffaloes

Old steam engines that burn wood or coal
Fishing trips and the swimming hole

Christmas songs that tell of Christ's birth
Peace proclaimed by angels to people on earth

Return of loved ones from far away
Comfort and solace when we pray
Peace and rest at close of day

Final Goodbye

My loved ones are gathered 'round me
As we say our final goodbyes,
And the sadness overtakes me
As the tear drops flood my eyes.

As I view their loving faces,
Fond memories crowd my mind,
And I recall the joy we shared
Along life's road of time.

And the years were filled with happiness
As we enjoyed them everyone.
There was our family's love and kindness,
And our friends who always stood by us
No matter what was said or done.

My dear wife and precious children--
A family so loving and fine.
How wonderful those years together--
How warm, how joyful and sublime.

How fast our lives were spent;
How quickly the years passed by...
It seemed we live only a moment
Before we must say goodbye.

Do not look on this frail body with pity;
It has endeared the ravages of time.
It was only on loan for a season
Until I can exchange it for a new one
Of God's more perfect design.

When I am gone,
Remember the kind words I have spoken
And never those words said in vain.
Because my only desire was to love you
And never to cause heartache or pain.

Now, please take my hands in yours
As I face death's evil night.
Then my thoughts will ever be with you
As my spirit takes its flight...

Forty Years Ago

There was a time when I was tall and handsome,
With hair black and wavy and eyes bright and bold.
My body was bronzed and muscular,
And the girls would stare in fascination
As down the street I'd stroll.
But now that's only a memory
Of forty years ago.

When young, I'd mesmerize the ladies
With my dark and brooding eyes
That seemed to look into their souls.
But now my eyes are dull and cloudy
With cataracts I'm told---
If I could only turn back the clock
To forty years ago...

My skin was once smooth and silky
With a healthy glow.
But now there's age spots on my hands,
And my face looks wrinkled and old.
I'll never look as good again
As Forty years ago...

My teeth were once straight and perfect,
And white as the fallen snow.
But now they're stained by coffee
To a dingy gold.
Lord, Please restore my youth
Of forty years ago…

In my youth, I'd play the guitar and sing
In a voice soft and low.
Then the girls would listen in rapture
And follow me wherever I'd go.
But Then I lost my hearing several years ago.
Now if a bomb went off nearby,
I wouldn't even know.
How I miss those good old times--
Of forty years ago…

My wife tells me I still got it
Just like in my youth long ago.
And everybody tells me
I don't look my age
Which gives me quite a glow.
But I think they're just being kind
Because I know I'm getting old,
And nothing works like it did--
Forty years ago…

Four-Leaf Clover

I found a lucky four-leaf clover today,
And I hope the legend is true.
Because I've had so much bad luck lately,
Some good luck should be due.

I wonder why so many things go wrong,
Why bad news at my door constantly calls.
It seems as if I didn't have bad luck,
I'd have no luck at all.

Sometimes,
I feel as if I'm under Joe Btfsplk's cloud
Or a Voodoo curse,
And no matter what I do,
My troubles just get worse.

Could it be that God is punishing me
For some past sinful trait,
Or was I just picked at random
By old Satan to torment and to hate?

Maybe
God is trying me as He did Job long ago,
To see if I'll be faithful,
No matter how bad things go.
And if I pass His test,
I hope He'll let me know.
And I hope He'll end this test real soon
Before my faith lets go.

Ghosts of Vietnam

Through long and sleepless nights,
I lie here in my bed while ghosts of Vietnam
Haunt my mind with fear and dread.
Young soldiers lying dead;
Many others crying out in pain.
On a battlefield in Nam,
Nothing will ever be the same...

Ambushed in the jungle,
My Buddy shot in the legs and head.
Over half of the platoon are wounded;
The other half are dead!

Mortar shells coming in;
Mines exploding all around!
Inflecting horrible wounds,
Body parts scattered on the ground!

Platoon surrounded by a minefield—
Afraid to move or breath!
Squad Leader stepped on a mine;
Legs blown off up to the knees!

Torture and brutality of a prison camp
After wounded and captured by Viet Cong!
The pain is so intense, but I must survive! --
My wife and kids need me back home.
On a starvation diet of one bowl of rice per day,
I am eating rats and bugs--trying to stay alive.

Will these ghosts of Vietnam ever leave me?
Will the mental anguish ever fade away?
Or will they always be three to haunt me...
Until my dying day?

Give Me a Star

Give me a goal to reach for
That's just beyond my grasp.
Then I'll try that much harder
To climb the ladder of success.

Give me a mountain to climb--
One that's steep, high and rough.
Then it will teach me patience,
And will make me strong and tough.

Give me a river to cross,
One that's swift, deep and cold.
Then I'll learn to swim or sink,
And give all that I have got
To reach my goal.

Give me a cross to bear
Like Jesus bore long ago.
It will make me meek and humble,
And bring peace to my weary soul.

Give me a star to reach for
So I will always do my best.
Let me do all that I can do,
And trust God to do the rest.

God, Family and Friends

In this world of greed and self-interest,
Sometimes we fail to see
That the most important things in
life are not wealth, fame and position,
But are God, family and friends--
So close to the hearts of you and me.

Fame is fickle and fleeting,
And wealth can be lost in a day.
Our health is uncertain and receding
And mostly a matter of genes they say.

But God is always near us--
Only a prayer away.
True friends will always assist us,
And our family will always stand by us--
No matter what other may say.

So, hold on to your faith and salvation,
And never from God go astray.
Always treasure your friends and family,
And keep them in your prayers every day.

God, Life, and the Universe

Some people say there is no God--
That He is only a hoax to ease our mind,
But to say the universe and Life "just happened"
Is a theory that is impossible to define.

The stars, the planets and galaxies,
All hung in space and balanced as a fine machine,
Could not have just happened by chance,
Or conceived by man in his wildest dream.

A miracle beyond the realm of chance,
It took a Master Engineer--a God Divine--
To conceive and create a universe
That leaves no doubt of its intelligent design.

The mystery of God, life, and creation,
Someday we will understand.
But for now, I choose to believe in God,
And that He created all things, including--
The universe, life, and man.

Of course,
Belief in God is a personal choice,
But beware, you could lose your soul!
All men will pray and cry out to God
When they feel death's evil cold.

God's Gift of Trees

Graceful in their summer leaves.
Home of birds, squirrels and bees,

Brilliant in their autumn gold.
Standing there for ages-old,

Firmly rooted in the ground,
Defying storms to blow them down.

With their branches lifted high,
Praising God as clouds drift by.

Catching every gentle breeze,
Sounds that put our minds at ease.

As the sun begins to rise,
Providing shade to soothe our eyes.

What wonderous beauty,
We would never see
If God had not made the trees.

Have You Ever Wondered

Have you ever considered how insignificant we are
When compared to universe or a distant star?
Or why God takes note of us at all,
Or why He listens when we call?

Of all the worlds in the universe,
Why is there water and air on the planet earth,
And food to eat and a temperature that's right
To support the needs of man and life?

Have you ever wondered where Heaven could be,
God's City of Gold by a crystal sea?
It could be near, or it could be far,
But I am sure it's out there on a shining star.

Have you ever wondered why there is suffering and death,
Or where our soul goes when we draw our last breath?
Will we be welcomed to Heaven's bright shore,
Or confined to earth to rise no more?

Have you ever wondered why Satan is here
To steal our souls and cause us fear?
Or why Jesus came to save our souls,
And to foil the plans of Satan's goals?

Have you ever wondered about the reason for it all;
About the creation of man and his subsequent fall;
About the temptation in the Garden and the original sin,
And the curse of death that shadows all men?

Whatever the reason, I believe God has a plan
To try by fire the mettle of man.
To see if he is worthy to ascend above all
By accepting God's Son to be redeemed from the fall.

He Loved This Land

While living in Ft Worth, TX, one Sunday afternoon, as was my custom, I was driving down a country road when I spotted a small family Cemetery. It was a peaceful scene with grave stones on either side of a small stream and live oak trees shading the graves. I stopped the car and got out to take some pictures and to read the grave stones. An inscription on one marker in particular caught my eye. The man had died at age 58 which was my age at the time. Needless to say, I thanked the Lord that by His grace I was able to read the inscription rather than to have passed away as this man had already. The inscription on the stone had the normal information and was followed by the statement: "He loved this land." It occurred to me then that, like so many other good men in this Country, he had spent a life-time living a decent, honest and responsible life, working hard every day to provide for his family. So, I think it goes without saying, that he loved not only his country, but he loved his family and his God. And now more than ever during this period of our history, we so desperately need more good men like him.

In the following poem, I wrote an inscription that I feel sums up how most honorable men feel about God, Family and their Country, and what words they may want engraved on their stone to mark their grave.

Underneath a (Virginia) sky
There dig my grave and let me lie.
Then let me rest peacefully
Until the Lord calls for me.
And on my stone engrave these words
So all who read them may understand:

He loved his God
He loved his family
He loved this land

Heaven

Somewhere across the universe
Beyond the stary seas,
God's heaven is out there shining--
Just waiting for you and me.

There in a golden city,
God's children will dwell with Him.
There will be no more pain or dying;
There will be no more strife or sin.

God's presence will light the city.
There will be no darkness or night.
And beside the crystal river,
Will bloom the trees of life.

There we will meet our Savior,
And look upon His face.
We will see His nail-scared hands,
And thank Him for his saving grace.

There around the golden throne,
We will gather one and all
And sing the victory song--
Christ redeemed us from the fall.

There we'll see again our loveones
That we lost so long ago.
We will hold them close to our hearts
And never let them go.

Ten thousand years will pass,
But it will seem only a moment in time.
There with the Lord and loveones,
How peaceful, How joyful, How sublime.

How Can We Measure the Cost

How many wars have been fought?
How many lives have been lost?
How many loved ones will never return?
How can we measure the cost?

How many infants have been aborted?
How many innocent lives have been lost?
How many children will never know love?
How can we measure the cost?

How many people are addicted to drugs?
How many promising lives have been lost?
How many of our children will never recover?
How can we measure the cost?

How deep in debt is our Nation?
How many jobs have been lost?
How many illegals have invaded our Country?
How can we measure the cost?

How many nations have been destroyed by Socialism?
How many millions of lives were lost?
How many radicals are hell-bent to destroy America?
How can we measure the cost?

Why is our Country in Chaos?
Why has national pride and honor been lost?
Why is there no leadership in Washington?
How can we measure the cost?

Why has God been forsaken?
How have our morals been lost?
How can our Nation recover its honor?
How can we measure the cost?

I'll Remember

When I am old
And my youth has been stolen by time,
But beautiful memories remain
That are stored in my mind.

I'll remember the glow of youth on your lovely face,
Your sweet loving ways and gentle grace.
I'll remember the glint of gold in your auburn hair,
Your beautiful grey eyes and the love shining there.

I'll remember your soft hands on my face;
The glow in your eyes as we embraced;
The tender words that came so natural to say
Each time I whispered your name,
And your soft lips that set my desires aflame.

And I'll remember the good times
When life together was so sweet and new.
But then I'll remember the hard times too
When duty called me to far-off lands,
And the "Goodbyes" were so hard to do.

I'll remember the sweet babies God gave us.
Their first steps, first words, their hugs so tight,
And their kisses wet on my face.
And most of all,
I'll remember the love that flowed like honey
In the youth of our lives,
In that wonderful time and place.

Then, when the flame of life burns low,
My last thoughts will be of you.
And I'll see you as I did long ago
When we were young and life was so fresh and new.
Then with my last breath, I'll whisper your name
And be thinking of you…

I'm Sorry

There were harsh, unkind words between you,
And in anger, you got carried away.
So you lost a Dear One's friendship
Because the words, "I'm sorry.",
Were just to hard to say.

You know how much you love him,
And you wanted him to stay.
But your pride and anger
Choked off the words, "I'm sorry.",
And you let him walk away.

There came a call from Heaven,
A conviction from God to pray.
But the words, "Dear Lord, Forgive me."
Were never pleaded,
And your soul was lost forever
When you passed away.

So, If you've hurt your loved one's feelings,
Or done wrong in anyway,
Please say these words and mean them,
"I'm sorry."
Before the close of day.

If I Could Change the World

If I could change the world
And make it over as I please,
All people would respect each other--
Regardless of race or creed.

Prejudice, discrimination and injustice
Would ever cease to be.
And intolerance, hate, and bigotry
No one would ever see.

I would banish all pain and suffering,
Heartache, death, and disease.
And hospitals, nursing homes and clinics--
Their need would cease to be.

There would be no gangs or violence;
No robbery, no forgery, no murder,
No crimes of any degree.
And no need for jails and prisons
Because everyone would be free.

No child would ever go hungry,
Be orphaned or in need,
And no mother would ever be in mourning
For a child lost to drugs, accident or disease.
No father, son or daughter would ever be killed in war
Because there would be no conflict or fighting
In my peaceful world.

There would be no religious intolerance,
No terrorism and bombings motivated by hate.
But all people would live in freedom
With the right to decide their own fate.

There would be no corruption in government
No bribes, no preference given to corporations,
The rich or people of any race.
But government would work fairly for everyone,
With honesty and integrity common place.

I admit this is a dream world created in my mind,
And doubtful it will happen given the evils of our time.
But we must always hope and pray
That the evils of man will cease,
That his goodness will prevail--
And the world can live in peace...

If I Could Read Your Mind

If I could read your mind,
Would there be thoughts of beauty, love and hope,
Or would your mind be vile and dirty,
And need washing out with soap?

If I could read your mind,
And your thoughts were changed to odors
as you think,
Would we smell the fragrance of roses,
Or would there be an awful stink?

If I could read your mind,
Would your thoughts be trite and petty,
Or noble, compassionate and kind,
With love for God and family...
Such thoughts have stood the test of time.

I am glad I can't read your mind,
And know only what you speak,
But remember, God can read your thoughts,
So, be careful what you think.

If I Could See Tomorrow

If I could see tomorrow,
What would I do differently today?
Would I be less critical, more generous,
And more patient with everyone
along life's way?

If I could see tomorrow,
How would I speak differently today?
Would my voice be softer,
More gentle, words kinder,
And what encouraging words would I say?

If I could see tomorrow,
How would I act differently today?
Would I be more humble,
Less prideful,
And more often kneel and pray?

If I could see tomorrow,
How would I view the world differently today?
Would I view God's creation with more wonder,
See goodness in people more clearly,
And hold family and friends
More precious in every way?

If I could see tomorrow,
How would I think differently today?
Would my thoughts be purer,
My heart and love be truer,
Or would temptation make me stray?

If I could see tomorrow,
And bad things stood in my way,
Would I have the courage to face them,
Or would I, like a coward, walk away?

In An Instant

In an Instant,
Our life on earth will be over,
And our journey here will cease.
The last breath will be taken,
And our soul will be released.

In an Instant,
There'll be no more pain and suffering,
No more heartache for loved ones gone before,
But we'll be joined together as a family
With no parting anymore.

In an Instant,
There'll be no more disease or dying,
No more hate, deceit or war.
There'll be only love and understanding,
And peace for evermore.

In an Instant,
Time want matter anymore
Because we'll spend a life eternal,
In the presence of the Lord and family,
On Heaven's golden shore.

In an Instant,
We must make a decision for Christ
If we would enter Heaven's door.
So, Let us all get ready now,
And plan to meet on Heaven's shore.

In Every Heart

In every heart, there is hope--
Hope for the future,
Hope for success,
Hope for health,
Hope for the best.

In every heart, there is love--
Love for family,
Love for friends,
Love for God,
Whose love never ends.

In every heart, there is faith--
Faith in God,
Faith in Mom and Dad,
Faith in our dreams
That we all have had.

In every heart, there is longing--
Longing for happiness,
Longing for love,
Longing for someone...
Now in heaven above.

In every heart, there is regret--
Regret for things said,
Regret for things done,
Regret for lost opportunities
That we could have won.

In every heart, there is hate--
Hate of cruelty and injustice,
Hate of disease and pain,
Hate of prejudice and intolerance--
Two evils--the same.

In every heart, there is joy--
Joy of family,
Joy of success,
Joy of life--
When we have done our best.

In every heart, there is fear--
Fear of the future,
Fear of the past,
Fear of failure,
Fear of death--at last.

Just a Boy Again

It doesn't seem that long ago,
That I was just a boy,
And life was fresh and new,
And I was
Wandering over hills and valleys
In search of fun and excitement,
As boys will often do.

How sweet those days of long ago,
When time was slow and free,
And every day was filled with wonder,
Of things we hear and see.

The old fishing hole was one of my favorite spots
For catching Horny Heads, Blue Gills, and Suckers.
If I was lucky and as a kid I was,
You could bet there would be fish for supper.

On Saturday,
My cousin and I would head for town
To watch a motion picture show.
The Cowboys were our heroes,
Fighting Indians, rustlers, and outlaws,
As they did in the West long ago.

In winter time,
When the weather turned cold,
My brothers and I would play hooky,
And go hunting rabbits in the snow.
We'd stay out all day tracking them down,
And maybe get a rabbit or two.
Then we'd head for home to sit by the fire
To warm our freezing feet,
Which by then would be turning blue.

Now, my boyhood days are passed,
And some of the wonderful things I loved to do.
But the Cowboys are still my heroes,
And I still love hunting rabbits
When the weather begins to cool.

Some may say,
"I'm trying to relive my boyhood",
While others will say,
"I am just a sentimental old fool."
But, foolish or not,
There's one thing I know:
That there seems to be a part of me
That just want let go,
Of those boyhood joys and pleasures
That I knew so long ago.

Just A Stranger

Some people say the end is near--
That Christ will return and men will fear.
They'll hide in caves and deep dark holes,
And cry out to God to save their souls.
But I made my peace a long time ago.
Now, I'm just a stranger passing through,
And I ain't got long down here below.

There's evil and sin on every hand,
And crimes of hate and greed across the land.
Lord, Be my Shepherd; keep me in your fold--
'Cause I'm just a stranger passing through,
And I ain't got long down here below.

Many dreary miles I've traveled,
Now, I am weak and tired and feeling old.
Lord, Walk beside me till the last mile I go--
'Cause I'm just a stranger passing through,
And I ain't got long down here below.

One can work and strive both day and night
To gain wealth and fame by wrong or right.
But what would you gain if you lost your soul?
'Cause you're just a stranger passing through,
And you ain't got long down here below.

Heartache, pain and trouble have plagued my way--
This life isn't easy; but we must hope and pray.
There's a heaven to gain, eternal life to know.
Keep your faith in the Lord; keep your eye on the goal--
'Cause we're all just strangers passing through,
And we ain't got long down here below.

Friends, With many of the coal mines in this area shut down, miners are out of work, and families are living on the edge. I have heard that over 1,000 have left the area. There are a lot of older miners around too who have worked in the coal mines all their lives, and some of them have no medical or retirement plan. Many of these miners have injuries and black lung and have been turned down for compensation. There are also a number of widows in the area whose husbands were either killed in the mines or died of coal mining related diseases. These people are now trying to survive on a small Social Security benefit and food stamps. It is a very sad situation, and in the following poem, I have tried to create an atmosphere that will imprint in your mind the desperate feelings that coal miners and their families have when there is no work, no money, and they are just trying to get by.

Just Trying to Get By

The rich are getting richer,
But I am getting poorer--
No matter how hard I try.
From dawn to dusk,
I'm doing my best
And just trying to get by.

The coal mines have shut down,
And we are all out of work.
With no money coming in,
It's hard times for our families,
Our neighbors, and friends.
They say good times are coming,
But it is pie-in-the-sky.
Sometimes, it ain't easy--
Just trying get by.

Disabled miners are all around;
Some with injuries and black lung,
But compensation was turned down.
On Social Security and food stamps,
It's hard to survive.
With no retirement or medical,
They are just trying to get by.

My old car needs work;
The tires are threadbare;
The engine is burning oil,
But there's no money for repair;
The insurance is due, but it's too high.
Sometimes, it's hard just trying to get by.

The house payment is due,
And the taxes are too.
My savings are all gone;
Oh, what can I do?
I'll sell my old truck,
And try not to cry...
No sacrifice is too great
When you are just trying to get by.

Winter is coming on,
And the kids need shoes.
This old house is so cold,
And my wife has the flu.
If I was an eagle,
From this place I would fly,
But there are responsibilities
That I can't deny.
So, I am longing for spring,
And just trying to get by.

Kids

Some kids are born wealthy;
Some kids are born poor,
And some are so lazy
That no amount of discipline will cure.

Some kids are born cute
While others are born plain,
And some kids have the knack
Of driving their parents insane.

Some kids are born large
While some are born small,
But to be born loved
Is the greatest gift of all.

Some kids are born weak
While some kids are born strong,
And some go through life
Where everything goes wrong.

Some kids are born slow
While others are quite wise,
And some are so loving,
They bring tears to your eyes.

Some kids are born skinny
While others are born fat,
And some are so spoiled rotten,
They turn out to be brats.

Some kids are born short
While others are born tall,
But to be born loved
Is the greatest gift of all.

Some kids are born white, yellow, red or black,
And while their personalities are all different,
And some may think odd,
There is one thing for sure--
They are all made by God.

Let Us be Thankful

Let us cherish each heart beat,
And each breath that we take.
Because God gave us life--
Let us give Him our thanks.

He created the universe--
The hills, the rivers and lakes,
And placed us on earth
Our homes to make.
Because God is great--
Let us give Him our thanks.

God's beauty in Nature is a delight to see---
The waterfalls, the flowers, the sky and trees.
He gave us a mind to wonder and to think.
Because God is good--
Let us give Him our thanks.

There are shoes on our feet
And clothes to wear,
And family and friends our love to share.
Our houses are warm,
And there is food on our plates.
Because God is gracious--
Let us give Him our thanks.

Let Your Conscience be Your Guide

In these times of easy virtue
When our values are being tried,
Stand firm for moral principles;
Let your conscience be your guide.

The world has lost its moral compass;
Evil is on a rising tide.
Never waiver from your convictions;
Let your conscience be your guide.

There're temptations all around us;
It's so easy to cheat and lie.
But dishonesty hurts us all,
Let your conscience be your guide.

When dealing with your neighbor,
Keep honesty on your side.
Always pay him back full measure;
Let your conscience be your guide.

There are poor and needy all around us
Who need our help to survive.
Are you generous with your time and money?
Let your conscience be your guide.

God gave us a mind to think and reason,
And a conscience to be our guide.
Always do what's right and honest,
And let your conscience be your guide.

Life's Record

When I come to the end of my journey,
And I can see life's setting sun,
Will I look back across the years
And be proud of what I have done?

Have I lived a life that mattered
by helping folks in need,
Or have I hoarded my time and money
And lived a life of selfish greed?

Can I point with pride to a desperate widow
and her children that I helped along life's way?
Can I count the number times I helped a brother
who from the fold had strayed?

Is there a record up in heaven of the times
I helped a friend or someone who was down and out?
Does the record reveal my life as generous
and caring, and of that, there is no doubt?

Did I feed the hungry and clothe the needy
who knocked upon my door?
And did I proclaim the story of Christ to
lost and desperate sinners and reveal
the love of God to a thousand souls and more?

Did the love in my heart never let me turn aside
from the old and feeble that I met along the way?
Did I treat them with honor and diginity and speak
words of kindness that brightened up their day?

Did I promote peace and harmony among my neighbors
and display the love of Christ for all the world to see?
Did I refraim from spreading rumors and gossip
that could hurt my friends and loved ones who
disagreed with me?

Did I honor and respect my parents who were
always there for me?
Did I call and visit them often their anxiety to relieve?
Did I ask the Lord to bless them in my every prayer,
And tell them how much I loved them and would
always care?

Did I treat my wife and children with tender
loving care?
When they needed love and understanding,
was I always there?
Did I listen to their problems and never turn away?
When asked for my help,
Did I always do my best to help in everyway?

Did I visit with orphan children and give them
of my love and time?
Did I encourage the depressed and lonely
to help ease their troubled mind?

Did I kneel at the bedside of the sick and dying
and offer up a prayer,
And ask the Lord to ease their pain and take
them home up there?

Did I comfort grieving loveones whose loss
was so hard to bear?
Did I offer words of sympathy that showed
how much I cared?

Has my life been one of honor and of value
that will forever last?
Or has it been only a tinkling symbol
and of sounding brass?

Has my life been real and earnest or only
one of pretend?
When at last I stand before the Lord,
Can my life's record I defend?

Lonely, Lonesome Feeling

There's a lonely, lonesome feeling
That comes with living alone...
No loving wife or children,
No one to share your home.

There's no warm embrace or smile
To welcome you at the door...
No one to share your dreams,
No one to share you joy.

No one has ever needed you
Or missed you when you're gone.
No hearts you've ever broken
Because no one your love has known.

There's no wife to call you Darling,
Or kids to call you Dad...
Because no loving sons and daughters,
You have ever had.

There's no Christmas toys to open,
Or birthdays to share...
No hugs and kisses from little daughters
With ribbons in their hair.

There's no hiking with your son
Along a mountain stream...
No fishing trips or camping
To add memories to your dream.

No words of love have been spoken
To an adoring wife...
No joy or happiness shared
Throughout your lonely life.

You've never opened up your heart
To a another soul.
Your love has been hoarded
Like a miser hoards his gold.

It's a sad and tragic feeling
When at last your days are few,
And there's no one there beside you
Whose love you know is true.
When no one has shared your life
Down through the lonely years,
And now you'll die alone...
With no one who weeps or cares.

Lord, Let Me Go Easy

When I have known the joys and pleasures
Of a life that has been long and sweet;
When I have climbed life's highest mountains,
But now I am old and weak---
Then Lord, don't let me suffer in a future
dark and bleak---
Just let me go easy; let me die in my sleep.

When my work here is finished,
And the last harvest has been reaped;
When my days have been numbered
And the count is now complete,
Then, Lord, Let me depart this world in peace---
Just let me go easy; let me die in my sleep.

When the nights are long and restless
And sad memories plague my sleep,
And I think of loved ones lost
And the tears that I have weeped--
Then Lord, Don't let me linger in the pain
so raw and deep--
Just let me go easy; let me die in my sleep.

When Death plays his evil game of hide and seek,
And there is no rest or peace,
Then, Lord, Let me cheat his cruel pleasure
And trust my soul to your keep---
Just let me go easy; let me die in my sleep.

When the suffering is so intensive,
And the pain I can't stand,
Grant me Oh, Lord your mercy
And the hope of every man--
Please walk beside me as I cross
Death's River deep--
Just let me go easy; let me die in my sleep.

When the Grim Reaper hovers near me,
And his shadow o'er me creeps,-
Then, Dear Lord, Be my Guide and Savior
And take me to that fair land I seek---
Just let me go easy; let me die in my sleep.

Lord, Count Me Down Slow

Our days on earth are numbered
As a story that is told,
But God does the counting;
He is in control.
So, a favor I pray, Dear Lord
You will grant me to know--
Please count me down easy...
Please count me down slow.

Lord, I know I am unworthy--
So often I have strayed from the fold.
But loving hearts will be broken
When from this earth I go.
Please count me down easy...
Please count me down slow.

Lord, My body is so weak and fragile
Wherein dwells my eternal soul.
Help me keep them both together—
More time with loved ones is my goal.
Please count me down easy...
Please count me down slow.

Loved ones are my greatest treasure
In this life I will ever know.
To keep them ever near me
Would be my greatest pleasure--
Lord, Please count them down easy...
Please count them down slow.

This life is so brief and tragic!
Many heartaches we must bear...
But there is a consolation
That in our hearts we share--
Someday we'll be together
In God's eternal fold.
But for now, Lord,
Please count us down easy...
Please count us down slow.

When my days have all been counted,
And my life on earth is through,
Lord, Please grant me one last favor--
Just meet me at the river,
And guide me home to heaven
To forever be with loved ones and you...

Lord, Turn America Around

Our Country is on the wrong road
That leads to a dead end of dissension and hate.
We have abandoned the principles of God
And the Founding Fathers that once made us great.
Lord, We need your help now; we can't wait!
Turn America around before it is too late!

Our Country is divided
With unrest and chaos in every State.
Demonstrations, looting, arson, race riots
And shootings are now common place.
Lord, We need your help now; we can't wait!
Turn America around before it is too late!

Our leaders are weak and corrupt
And feather their own nests.
They have sold out to Special Interests,
And honor and integrity has been put to rest.
Lord, We need your help now; we can't wait!
Turn America around before it is too late!

Our borders are wide open--
Allowing criminals, gangs and terrorist
To cross over at an astonishing rate,
While our citizens go unprotected
And are left to their own fate.
Lord, We need your help now; we can't wait!
Turn America around before it is too late!

Our prisons are full, and gangs, rioters,
Anarchists, and looters make our streets unsafe.
Young hoodlums assault, rob and rape,
But are slapped on the wrist and given a clean slate.
Lord, We need your help now; we can't wait!
Turn America around before it is too late!

Moral standards are ignored--so, anything goes.
Lord, Restore the National Conscience
And teach us to feel shame when our sins are exposed.
Lord, We need your help now; we can't wait!
Turn America around before it is too late!

Our kids have gone astray
With no discipline at home or in school.
Many are hooked on drugs and alcohol,
And think a wild, reckless lifestyle is cool.
Lord, We need your help now; we can't wait!
Turn America around before it is too late!

God's teachings are rejected in our schools,
Or even the mention of His name
Breaks our politically correct rules.
Our leaders have forgotten that our Country
Was founded on God's principles and laws--
To reject them now means our Country will fall.
Lord, We need your help now; we can't wait!
Turn Americas around before it is too late!

No nation can long endure
Without the blessings of God,
And all who forget Him will suffer that fate.
Lord, We need your help now; we can't wait!
Turn America around before it is too late!

In the following poem, I have attempted to make the case that man is only human and the inherent weaknesses which were there when God created us should be taken into consideration when we are judged for our mistakes. God surely knew even before He created man that he would be imperfect, and that he would fail his first test in the Garden of Eden. I am sure it is all part of God's plan to test his greatest creation (man) to see if he can overcome and endure the curse of death and all the pain, suffering and heartache that we all experience, and in passing the test, and by accepting His Son, Jesus, we could become the sons and daughters of God with the grand prize of eternal life. However, even though we are human, with all the weaknesses and imperfections, I am not insinuating that being human should be used as an excuse to give in to evil and committ any immoral or sinful act we desire. To please God, we must resist evil and live a decent and moral life as far as possible with His help...

Lord, We are Only Human

Lord, We are only human;
Don't judge us too harshly, I pray.
We are still a work in progress,
And hope to be perfect some day.

Some say that all people are evil,
But I don't see it that way.
Yes, we're often self-centered and selfish,
And sometimes to the dark side we stray.
But our love, goodness, and compassion
Can often be seen on display.

No doubt, some people are evil---
From God's love and mercy, they've strayed.
War, crime, death, and suffering are the result
That we see in the world today.

But, Lord, Don't hold us all in contempt
Or lose faith in the whole human race.
Most people are kind, generous and loving,
And of evil, there is seldom a trace.

Lord, You have set temptation before us
As a test of our character and will every day.
Sometimes we win, but sometimes we lose...
After all, we are only human...
Because, Lord, You made us that way.

Lost Inspiration

There was a time
When I could make words rhyme.
But now I've lost my infatuation
With words that please and give inspiration.

Once pleasant words filled my brain
Like spring flowers after an April rain.
Now those flowers have ceased to grow,
And pleasing words have ceased to flow.

What sad event or situation
Has caused me to lose my inspiration?
My wife and kids still love me, I know.
My finances and holdings have suffered no blow.
So, what could it be?
Please tell me if you know.

Could it be my health or the world situation
That has put me in to this state of depression?
Instead of my normal cheery self,
Have I turned into an anxious elf?

Maybe I'm in need of an overdue vacation
To reenergize my thoughts and inspiration?
Where could I go to get away from it all?
Some place where the crowds are not wall-to-wall...
The answer is obvious--Colorado!

Lost Moments

I could have said, 'You're beautiful
And lovely in every way."
But I was angry about some trivial matter,
And the moment slipped away.

I could have said, "I'm sorry."
But my pride got in the way.
Too many harsh words had been spoken,
And the moment slipped away.

I could have said, "I love you
Forever and a day."
And asked you to stay.
But my feelings had been hurt,
And the moment slipped away.

I could have said, "I need you
And don't ever go away."
But I felt to express it was a weakness,
And the moment slipped away.

So many times, because of our emotions,
Tender words are never spoken
That we could have expressed in so many ways.
Then we live our lives ever after to regret it...
Because the moments slipped away.

Love makes Everything Right

The morning is dawning,
And Oh, What a beautiful view!
The sun is shining, the skies so blue.
God is in His heaven, and He loves me and you.
So, let us pause and pray,
And thank the Lord for such a beautiful day.
Repeat: And thank the Lord for such a beautiful day.

There's a cool breeze from the sea,
And sparkling diamonds on the dew.
The birds are singing, and my heart is too!
Because , My Darling, I love you.
So, I'll just pause and pray,
And thank the Lord for such a wonderful day.
Repeat: And thank the Lord for such a wonderful day.

The moon is rising, the stars so bright.
The glow in your eyes is such a lovely sight.
And the love shining there makes everything right.
So, I'll just whisper a prayer,
And thank the Lord for such a perfect night.
Repeat: And thank the Lord for such a perfect night.

Man and Trees

A Man may live only a hundred years
Before he grows old and dies.
But a tree may live a thousand years--
Many times longer than you and I.

Our faces will tell our age
With wrinkles, spots and lines,
While trees add only another ring
To record the passage of time.

Our hair will turn gray with age,
And our bones become brittle and weak.
But trees only add more branches
And grow taller as to heaven they reach.

Some would say we are superior to trees;
We hear; we feel; we think.
But could it be that trees can hear, feel pain
And in their own way, they speak?

For who can deny the sweet music
We hear on a bright, sunny day
When a breeze caresses the leaves of a tree,
And the branches bow, bend and sway?

We know that man is greedy and selfish,
And only his own pleasure he seeks.
But trees are generous and giving--
Something for us all to consider--
As the next apple, plum or peach we eat.

I believe the following poem, in sacred and simple language, expresses the true meaning of marriage as God and Nature intended it to be:

Marriage

One woman,
One man
Go through life
Hand in hand.
Sacred vows
That seal our love,
Blessed by angels
And God above.

Tender words
Forever be,
Always spoken
By you and me.

Love that will
Forever bloom
Like the flowers
In May and June.

And may our home
Be ever blessed
By loving children
And happiness.

Memories Across the Years

When I think of loved ones lost,
Sweet memories bridge the lonely years.
Then I hear their voices and laughter,
And my eyes are filled with tears.

Dear faces that I loved and cherished...
Appear so lovely in my mind.
Bright eyes and happy smiles,
I then recall across the years of time...

Tender words of love and affection
Were so precious then, and more so even now--
Because their absence from our home
Cause tears of grief as our heads we bow.

How lonely are the years,
How broken are our hearts,
Without them here each day.
And time seems to have no meaning
As the hours, days, and years fade away...

Will time erase the pain and sorrow?
Will sad memories fade from view?
Only when we join them on a bright tomorrow
When our dearest memories of them--all come true...

Midnight Memories

Tossing and turning in my bed
As memories of you fill my head.
Thinking only of you since you've been gone,
And midnight memories want leave me alone.

When I close my eyes, your face I see,
And in my dreams, you still love me.
If only my dreams could all come true,
And I could lose these midnight memories of you.

Walking the floor and missing you...
Wondering what happened that made you untrue.
Was it something I did, or something I said?
How could you betray the love we once had?

The nights are so long--missing you.
Wondering if you miss me too...
Will time ever let me lose...
These midnight memories of you?

Chorus: Midnight memories of you,
Tossing and turning the whole night through.
Can't forget the love we once knew.
Just can't lose these midnight memories of you.

Morning and Night

I woke up this morning feeling so fine.
The night was so peaceful; my sleep was subline.
The sunlight in the window was shining so bright .
Thank the Lord for the morning.
Thank the Lord for last night .

Walked over the hill to see my Darling last night.
I kissed her sweet lips and held her so tight!
It made her so happy; her eyes were so bright!
Thank the Lord for the morning.
Thank the Lord for last night.

It was biscuits and gravy my Momma prepared,
With bacon and coffee that the family shared.
Then, off to Kings Mountain, the British to fight.
Thank the Lord for the morning.
Thank the Lord for last night.

The threats of Ferguson, we paid back in full.
We won the battle, and that was no bull!
With Patriots from the mountains we put them to flight!
Thank the Lord for the morning.
Thank the Lord for last night.

Then, home to my Darling, and soon we were wed.
Our vows made us one...so the preacher said.
In each other's arms, we spent the whole night,
And awoke to the morning with sun in the window
So golden and bright.
Thank the Lord for the morning!
Thank the Lord for last night!

My Final Journey

Goodbye, Dear Friends and Love Ones;
On this earth, I will see you no more.
I am bound for that beautiful city
On heavens bright, golden shore.

This life has been so happy;
Oh, how I would love to stay.
It breaks my heart to leave you,
But we will meet again someday.

How quickly has been my journey
Through this life here below.
It seems I had only begun to live
When I must say -- Goodbye-- and go.

But don't weep for me, Dear Love Ones,
I'll be waiting in heaven above---
Where we will ever be together
In that city of perfect love.

Now, let me dream of that city
That shines upon a hill.
Let me know the joys of heaven
When my eyes are closed and still.

Let me rest by that river
Where God's healing waters flow.
Let me drink from God's fountain
And peace forever know...

Let me walk up the streets of gold
With my loved ones gone before.
Let me eat of the tree of life,
And live for evermore...

Let me sing a song of victory
That no one has ever sung.
Let me look upon my Savior's face
And hear Him say, "Well done."

Then, I'll be waiting by the portal
To welcome friends and Loved Ones home.
What a joyful reunion we shall have—
There around God's golden throne...

My Heaven

Oh, They say there is a heaven
Where anyone can go.
And they say
There are mansions on the hills
And streets of purest gold.
But Lord, I am just a country boy,
And if it isn't too much trouble,
Please grant my humble plea---
Just build me a house in the country
Because that is where I long to be.

Lord,
My folks were poor mountain people.
My Dad was a miner of coal.
We had no fine house or luxuries;
We had no diamonds or gold.

Eleven kids in the family
Meant food would often get low.
Mom ensured we never got hungry,
But how she managed it,
I'll never know.

So, Lord, I'm sure you understand;
I don't want a fine mansion
Or walk on streets of gold.
Just an old gravel road
That leads me to my loved ones
And our home in the country--
That's my heaven;
That's where I long to go...

My Prayer

There's a prayer I like to say each morning
and at close of day:

Morning
Thank you, Lord, for keeping me
and my loved ones through the night.
Thank you for the strength to rise
and see the morning light.
To open up a window
and feel the morning breeze,
And look upon your world of
blooming flowers and trees.

Thank you for the morning sun
as it climbs the eastern sky,
And fills the world with light
as the day goes by.
And thank you for your only Son
sent down from heaven above
To fill the world with spiritual light
and His boundless love.

Keep us through this day Dear Lord
and evil far away.
Keep our loved ones in your care
and never let them stray.
Bless our children always.
May their lives be filled with light,
And keep them safe from all harm
against the coming night.

Evening

Now, at close of day, Dear Lord,
I give my thanks again.
Thank you for my loved ones,
my family and my friends.
And thank you for this day
and your love that never ends.

Please keep us
through another night, I pray,
Always in your loving care,
until the break of day.

And, Dear Lord,
If I should depart this life
sometime during the night,
My last prayer shall be:
Lord,
Always be with my loved ones,
my children and my wife,
And thank you once again
for so many blessings
and a wonderful life.

Getting new shoes when I was a kid was a time of excitement and joy. Now, kids, today, get new shoes and think nothing of it because they have so many pairs. Growing up back in the day, I had only one pair, and I went barefoot except in the winter time. I sometimes got new shoes in the Fall when starting back to school. But sometimes they were second hand or hand-me-downs depending on my family's financial condition. To me and I am sure to many of the older folks and the kids out there, getting new shoes is still a thrill... Hope you enjoy the poem...

New Shoes of Yesterday

There was a magic about new shoes
That brought happiness and joy
To a darling little girl,
Or a rambunctious little boy.

The leather was bright and shiny,
The soles unscratched and new.
Never been worn by anyone,
They were made just for you.

They came in your favorite colors--
For boys black and brown,
For girls red, white, and blue.
You couldn't wait to put them on
And show them off at school.

Some shoes required a "break-in",
Or they would pinch your toes.
But even if they hurt your feet,
No one would ever know.

And even in this modern day--
For kids or even older folks,
There is pleasure to be had--
When new shoes are bought
For the kids or even Mom and Dad.

No! It's Impossible!

Can one count the blades of grass that grow upon a hill,
Or the number of leaves that fall during Autumn's chill?
Can the grains of sand be numbered on a beach by the sea,
Or the total of birds that fly in the skies wild and free?
No! It's impossible! Some things are just impossible!

Can we corral the galaxies that spin around in space,
Or number the stars that have exploded and never
left a trace?
Can raindrops be added up during a summer rain,
Or lightning strikes prevented on the mountains
and the plains?
No! It's impossible! Some things are just impossible!

Can we drain the oceans and count the fish in the seas,
Or number the snowflakes falling during a winter freeze?
Can ants and bugs be contained that crawl upon the earth,
Or kind words assigned a value of what they are really worth?
No! It's impossible! Some things are just impossible!

Can scientists count the atoms in our bodies
Or the cells in our brains?
Have they found a way to explain human actions
When greed and hate are unrestrained?
Can one explain the mystery of birth or the curse of death,
And where our souls go when we draw our last breath?
No! It's impossible! Some things are just impossible!

Can man control the weather or stop a tornado in its tracks,
Or travel back in time to verify historical facts?
Is there a way to value friendship or a friendly smile,
Or compute the grief of a Mother when she has lost a child?
No! It's impossible! Some things are just impossible!

Can the love of God be explained when He gave His only son--
To redeem the souls of men for the evil they had done?
Can Christ be understood as He suffered on the cross,
And gave His life for us because we all were lost?
No! It's impossible! Some things are just impossible!

Oh, I Must Go Back

Oh, I must go back to all the old places
And recall in my memory the names and the faces--
Of neighbors and friends and loved ones so dear...
Yes, I must go back and recall once again
Those wonderful years...

I'll visit the old school ground where I played as a boy,
And remember my class mates--the shared fun and the joy.
So many have passed on down through the years,
But their young faces I see through the sadness and tears.

I'll fish in the rivers and hunt in the woods,
And recall my youth when life was good.
I'll look up old friends who are still around;
We'll talk of good times and the happiness we found.

I'll walk the old paths by the hills and the streams,
And think of years past, my goals and my dreams...
How blessed I am with the Dear Woman I love,
And our loving children--God's gifts from above.

The church will be there in the valley
Where we would gather to pray--
Surrounded by loved ones and friends,
Who have now long passed away.

As I read their grave stones,
In memory, their faces will appear,
And I'll recall their smiles and laughter,
And words of love...so precious to hear.

The old homeplace is gone; it burned long ago,
But sweet memories remain of our dear family fold.
There was laughter and joy, sadness and pain,
But how I wish I could be with my family again.

Yes, I must go back to that place long ago,
Before my memories fade, for now I am old.
How long I will live, God only knows,
But when my time comes, return me I pray--
To the church in the valley, and there dig my grave,
And there let me lay--
Surrounded by loved ones and friends--
Who have long passed away...

Oh, So Long Ago

In the spring of our lives
When you were so young and shy;
And I was so eager and bold,
We pledged our love would never die,
But that was...Oh, So long ago.

In the summer of our lives,
Our love would blossom and grow.
We spent so much time together,
And in those moments we knew
We were meant for each other,
But that was...Oh, So long ago.

Now, a life-time has passed,
And the cold winter of our lives
Has left us weak and old.
But in our hearts the love still burns
With a beautiful glow
Because time can never dim the
Wonderful love we knew...
Oh, So long ago.

Oh, Glorious Morning

Oh, Glorious morning when Christ returns,
We'll meet Him in the sky.
The dead will rise, we'll all be changed,
And no one will ever die.

Oh, Wonderous morning when Christ returns
With His angel band--
His promise kept, resurrection sure,
Salvation for every man!

Chorus:
Oh, Blessed morning when Christ returns,
We'll see His nail-scarred hands!
Such love that made Him die for us
To save the souls of man.

Oh! joyous morning when Christ returns,
Oh, How the tears will flow--
To see our loved ones once again
That we lost so long ago!

Oh, Triumphant morning when Christ returns,
The victory has been won!
We've stayed the course; we've kept the faith,
And Christ will say will done.

Paths of Life

Lord, If I wasn't me,
Then who would I be?
Was it by chance that I was born,
Or did you plan my birth
For one bright Sunday morn?

Am I unique to this place and time,
Or just a standard model
On your assembly line?
Was my life ordained
For something great,
Or will chance decide my life and fate?

Did you instill in me a spark divine?--
A gift or talent to bless mankind?
Or am I just an average Joe
On the road of life---
Fated to achieve nothing of note
In this world of strife?

Lord, Did you take special care
To form my brain
That I may win wealth and fame?
Or did you decide for me
A humbler role
Of service and sacrifice
To cleanse my soul?

Has success and greatness
Been for me ordained,
Or will I spend my life
On this earth in vain?

There is a mystery here
That we don't understand--
Does God preordain the lives of man,
Or is it up to us which path we take
And make the choices that decide our fate?

Peace Like a River Flowing

My life was lost and wasted; no peace did I know.
Then Jesus came and found me and revived my weary soul.
He gave me peace and comfort that I had never known.
Now there's peace like a river flowing deep within my soul.

Chorus:
There's peace like a river flowing that everyone should know.
Just give your life to Jesus, He'll make you free and whole.
He's reaching out to save you and welcome you to the fold,
And peace like a river flowing will flow into your soul.

Christ bore our grief and sorrow a long time ago.
Upon a Cross at Calvary, He died to save our souls.
There's mercy, grace and pardon, and you'll never walk alone,
And peace like a river flowing will flow into your soul.

Our lives are quickly passing; the future no one can know,
But Jesus has the answer for our troubles here below.
Just call upon His name, He'll welcome you to the fold,
And peace like a river flowing will flow into your soul.

Lift up your eyes to heaven and open up your soul.
Embrace Christ's love and mercy; He'll give you joy untold.
There's room for all of God's children in His heavenly home,
And peace like a river flowing will flow into your soul.

Peace

I want to flee from all the noise and stress,
And live free with God and Nature in perfect bliss.
I want to go where there's a peaceful scene,
And while away the day
On the grassy bank of a sparkling stream.

I want to be at ease with sun and sky,
And watch an eagle as it flies on high.
I want to hear a Blue Bird sing,
And see the Swallows fly
When they return in spring.

I want to hike along a wild mountain stream,
And see the flowers and trees awaken in spring.
I want to see a sunrise gleam
Across the snow of a Rocky Mountain scene,
And feel the breeze as it passes by,
And look forever into a clear blue sky.

I want to feel the misty rain
As Nature waters the flowers in early spring,
And smell their fragrance on the morning breeze,
As it makes my mind feel at ease.

I want to see a rainbow play
In waterfall mist and ocean spray,
And see the waves rise and dip,
And watch the wind
As it fills the sails of a Clipper Ship.

But can any of these earthly scenes ever compare
To heaven and all its beauties up there?
With the Tree of Life beside the Crystal Stream,
It will be more beautiful than we can ever dream.

Maybe I could go hiking with the Lord up there,
Along the River of Life and up the Golden Stairs,
Across the Sea of Glass to the Father's throne,
And be there with my loved ones...
Forever in peace at home.

People are Funny That Way

As we pass through this life,
We are apt to meet many funny people
as we walk down the street.
Some will smile and say, "Hello"
While others will only "nod".
But others will give you the evil eye,
Or rudely stare as if you are something odd.
But in the final analysis, what can one say--
Only that people are funny that way.

Some people will be gracious and wish you well,
But others will be jealous and hope you fail.
Some will rejoice at your good fortune and success
While others will be resentful that you are blessed.
But in the final analysis, what can one say--
Only that people are funny that way.

You will pass the helpful, generous and kind,
But others will be contentious and judgmental
most of the time.
Beware of the self-righteous who condemn
and point fingers at us all.
They have forgotten that Christ taught
love and forgiveness to save man from the fall.
But in the final analysis, what can one say--
Only that people are funny that way.

You will meet the quiet, peaceful and meek,
As well as the mean and cruel who bully the weak.
A few will be rich, but many will be poor.
You will hear many talkers, but see very few doers.
But in the final analysis, what can one say--
Only that people are funny that way.

You will shake hands with some preachers,
Who say they have found the true path--
that only they know,
And they will show you the way if you'll give
them some dough.
They live in fine mansions, drive fancy cars
And fly in jet planes wherever they go.
But if you follow their path, you'll end up below.
But in the final analysis, what can one say--
Only that people are funny that way.

If lucky,
You will encounter the congenial and friendly
that never frown.
They are always happy and humorous,
And fun to be around.
But then there are the complainers and whinners
That are never happy unless they are
spreading lies and gossip all over town.
But in the final analysis, what can one say--
Only the people are funny that way.

By chance you may meet some rich and selfish
who live in their own world of lavish content--
Never helping the poor or contributing a cent.
Love and compassion is not their style.
They have never learned giving enriches the soul
And makes life worthwhile.
But in the final analysis, what can one say--
Only the people are funny that way.

Just waiting for the gullible
Will be the deceivers, pretenders and con-artists,
Who are always looking for prey.
They'll take all your money and be on their way.
Watch out for the "Gold Diggers"--
Because one can be sure that the love
they confess--
Is only a ruse to get your house, your car
and all you possess!
But in the final analysis, what can one say--
Only that people are funny that way.

It seems we each have our own peculiar ways.
Be they good or bad,
It is normal for the human race I'd say,
Or could it be that God needed a laugh
And made us that way.
But in the final analysis, what can one say--
Only that people are funny that way.

Pictures in My Mind

There are pictures in my mind
And scenes from long ago--
Of events, people and places
And of the family fold.

The pictures recall sweet memories
Of a family so loving and true,
And of gatherings at the old home place
And of friends that we once knew.

Some pictures are in full color,
While others are faded black and white,
But the pictures I see of love ones
Light up the chambers of my heart
And make the scenes so bright.

There are carefree scenes of childhood
And of barefoot kids at school--
Where we were taught reading, writing
and arithmetic,
And where we learned the *Golden Rule*.

How precious those scenes of Mom and Dad
And of the family fold,
And the celebration of holidays, birthdays,
weddings and births--
That warmed our hearts and souls.

Then I see pictures of old girl friends
And of that special Sweetheart,
Who later would become my bride--
Because we were married in the spring time,
And now her picture is forever in my mind.

Precious Things

Precious things that God gives us
That enhance and enrich our lives---
Like family, friends, and lived ones
That make this life worthwhile.

Precious Father, loving Mother
Whose love is so strong and sure.
They will always be there for us
Just as long as life endures.

Cherished time we spend together
As a family so devoted and close.
Loving arms that enfold us
When we need their love the most.

Devoted wife, adoring husband,
Our love will grow through the years.
And will bind us ever closer
As we share life's joys and tears.

Precious children that God gave us,
Oh, how we'd love to keep them home,
But too soon they will leave us--
To start families of their own.

Encouraging words that are spoken
That relieves our pain and fear.
And the comfort that we feel
When our children are safe and near.

Kindness and support from our friends
That helps us endure life's heavy load.
And their loyalty and understanding
As we travel down life's rocky road.

Precious promise from Christ, the Lord
Of life beyond this veil of tears.
And we will see again our loved ones
That we miss and hold so dear.

Reflections on Age and Time

I look around, and what do I see--
Everybody looks younger than me.
I visit the cemetery with fear and dread
Because most people my age are already dead.

It dosen't seem that long ago
That I was young and in my prime
With a young wife and kids
And no worries about age or time.

Then one morning, I looked in the mirror
And what did I see--grey hairs on my head
where none used to be.
Where did all of those years go;
Why did time have to fly?
We live only a moment and then we must die.

From birth to about 20, time passes so slow.
We can't wait to grow up and start our own show.

From 20 to 40, we don't even notice time passing by.
Because we are so busy living, we don't even try.

Then from 40 to 60, time streaks by in a flash--
Like a speeding Bullet Train on the wrong track
And bound to crash.

From 60 to 80, times flashes by with the speed of light--
Like a Space Ship in warp drive
That we don't even notice till it is gone out of sight.

So now I am past 80--how did I live so long?
My kids are all grown, and have kids of their own.
My wife still looks young, but I'm looking old.
She will probably outlive me by 20 years or so.

I've got a lot of health problems,
But there is no need to complain.
They come with old age; It's just a natural thing.

At my age,
I know the Grim Reaper is looking me over--
His next victim to claim.
But with the Lord's help, I'll fight till the end,
And I hope you will do the same.

Road Along the River

There's a road along the river
Where the weeping willows grow,
And the sycamores cast their shadows
O'er the water as it flows.

Early morning fog drifting on the water;
Sunbeams dancing in the pools,
Star diamonds flashing in the rapids,
And the breezes so fresh and cool.

Wild flowers blooming everywhere--
Bright yellow, blue and red.
Golden sunshine sprinkled on the trees,
Cotton ball clouds and blue skies overhead.

Worries and cares have all vanished
As I view the tranquil stream--
A fish eagle soaring down the river;
A blue heron fishing in the shallows,
Could there be a more peaceful scene?

Each bend of the river
Reveals more gorgeous views.
There's a waterfall on a side stream
That plunges into a pool--
With rainbows in the mists
Flashing red, gold, and blue.

Come hike with me, Dear Friends;
It's a hike you will approve--
Down the road along the river
Where the scenes are so beautiful
And the breezes so fresh and cool.

Safe at Home

This old world is full of danger,
And we worry about our kids
As we sit here by the phone.
Then we hear familiar footsteps
And the sweetest words this side of heaven:
"Mom, Dad, We're home."

When our son went off to war,
Long months we worried alone.
Then one day, we heard familiar footsteps,
And the sweetest words this side of heaven:
"Mom, Dad, I'm home."

If we live to be a hundred,
And we're sitting here all alone,
We'll still be listening for familiar footsteps,
And the sweetest words this side of heaven:
"Mom, Dad, We're home."

Even when we move up to heaven
And we're sitting there by the throne,
We'll be listening for familiar footsteps,
And the sweetest words ever heard in heaven:
"Mom, Dad, We're home."

Shadow on a Wall

In this life of strife and trouble,
Many trials will test us all.
Can you face the tests with courage,
Or, are you just a shadow on a wall?

One can go through life and make a difference,
Or live a life that is trivial and small.
But if you would be remembered with affection,
Don't become, just a shadow on a wall.

Are you filled with self-importance,
Have you become a know-it-all?
Remember, "Pride goeth before destruction,"
And you become, just a shadow on a wall.

Honor and integrity define our character,
And mercy is a quality valued by all.
Are these qualities part of your character,
Or have you become, just a shadow on a wall?

When you near the final exit
And the curtain begins to fall,
You'll be glad you made a difference,
And were not, just a shadow on a wall.

Shirley Darling

Oh, I love you, Shirley Darling.
Would you share your life with me?
Oh, I want you, Shirley Darling,
For my loving wife to be.

Do you love me, Shirley Darling?
Please return my love so true.
Do you want me, Shirley Darling
For your loving husband too?

Oh, I love you, Shirley Darling.
Would you share your life with me?
Oh, I want you, Shirley Darling
For my loving wife to be.

We were married in the spring time
When the flowers were in bloom,
And the birds were singing sweetly
In the beautiful month of June.

Oh, I love you, Shirley Darling.
I'm so glad you now are mine.
We will walk through life together--
Through the storms and sunshine.

Then there was a little baby
With bright eyes so big and blue--
And a smile that melts my heart
Because my Darling, She looks like you.

Oh, I love you, Shirley Darling.
I'm so glad you now are mine.
We will walk through life together--
Through the storms and sunshine.

Sleep

How restful the sleep of a working man,
Who earns his bread with his own two hands?
His days are filled with labor and sweat;
He welcomes the night as a time of rest.

How peaceful the sleep of an honest man,
Who for an honorable life he firmly stands.
His conscience is clear as he closes his eyes,
Because his life is one of integrity
And freedom from lies.

How blessed the sleep of a righteous man,
Who serves the Lord as best he can.
He fears no evil that prowls the night,
And sleeps soundly until the morning light.

How refreshing to awaken from a good night's rest,
And look upon God's world and know we're blessed.
To feel renewed in body and soul,
And ready for the day, whatever it holds.

There's a final sleep that we all must take,
But it will seem only a moment before we awake!
There in the presence of the Lord
On heaven's shore with our loved ones forever more...

Friends, I have heard it said that "One cannot know real happiness unless you have first experienced the depths of sorrow, or that we must see the face of evil before we can recognize the purity of goodness, or that there can be no victory without struggle." I am sure there is much truth in these statements, but as we experience the grief, sorrow, pain and troubles of this life, we can't help but wonder why God allows it all to continue. In the following poem, I ask some of these questions and give my own possible answer.

Someday

Someday down this road of life,
We'll know the reason for the chaos and strife...
Why there's is so much grief and pain,
And why God lets things happen
That no one can explain.

Someday we'll see through this veil of tears
And understand all the doubts and fears.
Then, we'll fathom the reason for war and death,
And why evil seems to always win...
Even when we do our best.

Someday a light from heaven will shine
And reveal God's plan so clear in our mind.
We'll see that this life is but a test,
And if we pass, we'll forever be blessed.

So, shall we challenge God's plan for man,
Or patiently wait and someday understand...
That He knew best for our lives on earth
And prepared us well for all heaven is worth?

Somethings/Sometimes

Somethings I regret;
Somethings I don't.
Somethings I will do,
But somethings I want.

Somethings I have said,
I said in haste.
Somethings I avoided,
I wish I had faced.

Somethings I experienced
In the hard school of fate.
Somethings I have learned,
But I learned them too late.

Somethings I have said,
Caused angush and pain.
Some decisions I made,
I wish I could change.

Somethings I know now,
I wish I knew then.
Some people I once disliked
Are now my friends.

Sometimes it's better
To forget and forgive.
Sometimes it's better
To live and let live.

Sometimes I'm deceptive
But try never to lie--
Because every lie that we tell,
We'll regret when we die.

Sometimes I am happy;
Sometimes I am sad.
Sometimes I am good,
But sometimes I am bad.

Sometimes I'm self-centered;
It's all about me.
Sometimes I'm so proud
The truth I can't see.

Sometimes I remember;
Sometimes I forget.
Some clothes that I buy
Seem never to fit.

Sometimes I am early,
But I'm seldom late.
But a Doctor appointment
Is one thing I hate.

Sometimes I'm sick,
And sometimes I'm well.
Sometimes life is easy,
But sometimes it's hell.

Sometimes I love,
But sometimes I hate.
Sometimes I regret,
But sometimes it's too late.

Sometimes I feel old;
Sometimes I feel young.
Sometimes I feel smart,
And sometimes I feel dumb.

Sometimes I lack confidence--
Other times I have too much pride.
Sometimes I am arrogant--
Other times snobbish and snide.

Somethings I want;
Somethings I don't.
Somethings I get,
And then I don't want.

Somethings we neglect
And leave up to fate,
But take no chances with your soul...
Make peace with the Lord --
Before it's too late!

Springtime

There's a pleasure in the springtime
Like no other time of year--
When the flowers are in bloom
And the skies so bright and clear.

It's a time of honey bees and butterflies,
Of rainbows and the gentle rain.
A time of peach blooms and apple blossoms
As the grass and trees are turning green.

It's a time to enjoy the beauty of Nature
And awaken to the birds as they sing;
To see the miracle that God proclaims
As new life is born on every mountain,
valley, and plain.

It's a time to climb a mountain high;
To view the valleys, hills, and sky;
Then hike along a mountain stream,
And see the waterfalls as they gleam;
To smell the fragrance of all things new,
And see the rainbows in the morning dew.

Now, we can forget the wind and snow;
Dream new dreams and set new goals;
Forget our doubts and seek new truths,
And cast off the gloom of winter blues.

Because the birds are singing in the trees,
And the fragrance of flowers is on every breeze.
The swallows are returning from far away
With the pleasure of bright and sunny days.

It's a time for sweethearts to start a new life...
To get married and become husband and wife.
And as you speak those sacred words, "I do.",
Remember, marriage is forever, so always be true.

So, awaken world, springtime is here!
Winter is gone for another year!
This is a season for joy and mirth...
Look around and rejoice;
God has made a beautiful new earth!

Stars in the Night

Like sparkling diamonds in the night,
The stars appear in magnificence light.
Placed above by God's own hand,
Wondrous lights for the joy of man.

As they twinkle in the night
Providing mariners a guiding light.
For millennia they have shown the way
For men who brave the ocean waves.

Each star a world so far away
With folks like us, we cannot say.
But our restless spirit drives us far
To find out who our neighbors are.

Billions of stars send light our way,
And reach out to God as if to pray.
Lighting up the universe at night,
Proclaiming to all that God is light.

Somewhere out there, we know not where,
God's Heaven is shining on a brilliant star,
A city of gold by a crystal sea,
Just waiting there for you and me.

Take it Slow

The world seems in a hurry
As people rush from place to place.
In cars, planes and trains,
Everyone seems to be in a race.
But life could be less hectic
As down the road we go
If we'd only take our time,
And learn to take it slow.

It seems we're always busy
And the rat race never slows.
Work and family all demand our time,
And we're always on the go.
But our lives could be less stressful
If we'd only pace ourselves
And learn to take it slow.

Some people rush around
And raise a lot of dust.
You'd think they ruled the world
Considering all the fuss.
Sometimes it makes you wonder…
Is it just for show?
Because we know they'd get more done
If they'd only take it slow.

Rome wasn't built in a day,
And the Pyramids took 20 years we're told.
So, tell me what's the rush;
I'd really like to know.
Ancient people achieved great things
Because they learned to take it slow.

Our days on earth are numbered;
God alone decides how long we go.
But those days can be more peaceful
If we take time to smell the roses
And learn to take it slow.

Take it with a Smile

This life isn't easy,
But take it with a smile.
For all the things that are bad,
There are many more worthwhile.

Look on the bright side;
It will shorten every mile.
The road of life will be less bumpy...
If you take it with a smile.

Say a friendly "Hello" to everyone;
Show them that you got style.
Everything in life will be more pleasant...
If you take it with a smile.

When nothing seems to go right
And everything seems a trial--
Remember,
It takes a storm to make a rainbow,
So, just take it with a smile.

When troubles overwhelm you
And friends forsake you all the while;
Just say a little prayer,
And you can take it with a smile.

When death hovers near you
And you have gone your last mile,
Just put your trust in the Lord
And leave this world with a smile.

Tell Me You Love Me

Tell me you love me;
Tell me you care.
Call me your Daring...
Forever, My Dear.

Whisper love to me;
Say sweet words in my ear.
Tell me you adore me...
Forever, My Dear.

Tell me you want me
In words soft and clear.
Tell me you need me...
Forever, My Dear.

Let me kiss your lips tender
And hold you so near--
That I may hear your heart beating...
Forever, My Dear.

Terms of Endearment

Terms of endearment are easily spoken
To love ones we hold dear,
But so often we neglect to say them
And to make our feelings clear.

How precious the sound of, "Darling"
To a husband or a wife
When spoken with love and feeling
As they face together the trials of life.

From our children,
A hug and kiss are always welcome
As we greet the morning light.
And don't forget to say I love you
When you kiss them all goodnight.

A nice gift will surely bring a smile
To the face of that special someone
That you have loved for such a while.
Whether it be flowers, candy or diamonds,
It matters not the cost;
It is only the thought that counts,
And not the gain or loss.

Gentle words of sympathy softly spoken
To a friend who has suffered a love one's loss
Will bring relief and comfort
And help them endure the pain it cost.

Terms of endearment, like rays of sunshine,
brighten up our lives.
Given with warmth and feeling,
They make us realize--
That love and support are always near us--
No matter how dark the skies.

Texas Rain

How exciting to feel the soft falling rain
After months of drought on the Texas plains.
Now the fields and pastures will all turn green
As water flows again in the rivers and streams.

As a rainbow appears in the western sky,
The rains fill up the wells that ran dry.
The lakes, stock ponds and springs will all revive,
And the blooms of the Bluebonnet and Paintbrush
Will come alive.

The burned over prairie will explode with new life,
And the Texas Rancher
will celebrate with his children and wife.
Again, there will be abundant water for man and beast
Because
The rains have finally brought much prayed for relief.

The dust will be settled,
And the air will be fresh and easier to breathe.
With the fragrance of sage
On a welcoming breeze.

If God would bless Texas with a little more rain
And a little less heat,
It would be a paradise for man as well as his beasts.
But I guess Texans wouldn't want anything to change
Because hardships have made them Bull-leather tough,
And as a matter of pride, they think that's enough.

TGIF

Friday is the day of the week that I love best.
As I look forward to the weekend and much needed rest.
Forget about work, I can sleep late.
Or just lie around the house, or take the family to the lake.

Saturday is family shopping day
To stock up on groceries and good things to eat.
Later we'll swing by the Mall
If the kids need new clothes or shoes for their feet.

And on the way home,
We'll all be hungry, and it'll be time to eat.
So we'll stop by McDonalds or a pizza place
For a fast-food treat.

The wife may have some "Honeydos" lined up,
Like cleaning out the garage or cutting the grass.
But my mind is on fishing and catching a big bass.
Those honeydos will just have to wait
Because I need some free time---
To get out there in Nature and let my nerves unwind.

After church on Sunday,
We'll take a ride in the country,
And have a barbecue at the lake.
The kids can go Swimming,
And I'll do the cooking to give the wife a break.

Well, the weekend is about over, and we had a lot of fun.
Had some quality time with the family and playing in the sun.
Hope the workweek flies by and it's over and then---
It's TGIF and the weekend again.

The Book of Life

Our lives are like a book
With chapters added year by year.
Through words, deeds and actions,
We write each chapter clear.

Some pages God will write
With His indelible pin--
Like when we are born,
How long we live,
And how our story ends.

How sweet the pages filled with love--
Of God, friends and love ones too.
There are weddings, births and family
That make our dreams come true.

We have one chance and only one
To write each chapter new.
We will pass this way only once
Before our journey is through.

When your Book of Life is finished,
How will the story read?
Are pages filled with love and kindness,
Or only cruelty and greed?

The Case for Man

If I could say prayer
That would open heaven's door,
I would pray for peace on earth
And forever the end of war.

I would plead for the sick and suffering
And for healing across the land--
That all diseases would be cured
And all evil on earth be banned.

I'd make the case for justice
That the curse of death be lifted
Because of one man and woman's sin,
That all people would be pardoned
And eternal life restored again.

How can a man ever sin enough
To burn forever in the fires of hell?
Why condemn the whole human Race
Because one man and woman failed?

As mortal parents,
We would never condemn our children
To eternal pain and fire
No matter how many rules they break
Or how many mistakes they make.

Since the dawn of creation,
Man has endured constant trouble
With pain, sorrow, and strife---
Then to earth he returns
At the end of his short life.

Man's life and fate seems so unjust
By any standard of fairness or law...
Especially from God the Father,
Who is more compassionate than us all.

These are questions we can't answer,
And God has not chosen to make it clear.
But don't you think we deserve an answer
Considering the pain and sorrow we endear?

The Coal Miner

It's up before dawn and off to the mine.
Never home before dark, I seldom see sunshine.

This hole in the ground is dark as a tomb,
But my carbide lamp will banish the gloom.

The work is hard loading this coal;
The hours are long, and the wages are low.

The Boss is always riding my back.
Demanding more work, he never cuts me any slack.

This old coal mine is dirty and cold.
If the ceiling falls on me, darkness will swallow my soul.

I wonder how many men have died in this mine.
With dangers all around, death can pounce any time.

There's coal dust, rock dust, and poison gas;
The dangers are real--
If a cave-in don't get me, black lung will!

There's coal dust in my nose, my eyes and my hair.
Before this day is over, I'll be black as a bear.

For forty years I've worked in this mine.
I've breathed so much coal dust that now it's a fact--
If you were to cut me, my blood would run black.

A miner's wife's work is never done it seems.
There's clothes to be mended, kids to be tended,
And supper to be fixed of cornbread and beans.

On payday,
I'll spend all my money at the company store.
The prices are high, and there's one thing for shor'
They'll have all my wages before I can get out the door.

For most of my life, I've worked in this mine.
And someday, Lord willing, a better job I'll find.
But for now, I'll have to stay.
Got a family to feed, gotta keep on earning my pay.

Dedicated to my Dad, who worked in the coal mines of SW Virginia for over 40 years.

The Common Touch

Some folks are blessed with riches,
But the poor we have with us always.
And somehow, it doesn't seem just.
But only by respecting everyone
Can we show the *common touch*.

Some people parade their wealth
And are known as the upper crust.
While some give freely; others are greedy--
It's quite clear who has the *common touch*.

We all have known loving, caring people
That were raised poor like us;
But later became rich and wealthy,
And turned into a snob and miser,
And lost the *common touch*.

A man can spend his whole life in luxury
And ignore the poor if he must,
But when he stands before Christ in judgment,
He'll hear these fateful words...
"You didn't show the *common touch*."

The Destiny of Man

What worth has a man?
What value his soul?
He spends his days,
And then he grows old.

What did he accomplish?
What did he gain?
He accumulated no wealth,
He knew no fame.

From birth to death, his life is spent
Laboring for food, clothes and rent.
If lucky, he finds a loving wife
To love and cherish some of his life

When at last the curtain begins to fall,
Can he look back with pride
And great accomplishments recall?
Or was his time on earth spent in vain?
Will anyone long remember his name?

Or, did he fulfill a beautiful plan
That God has ordained for the destiny of man?
To ascend above this earthly state--
And fly with the angels through heaven's gate.

The Face in The Mirror

The face in the mirror tells a story,
And it's written there plain to see
In laugh lines of happiness
And wrinkles of misery.

The reflection in the mirror
Is the face everyone can see.
But hidden behind the face,
Is there a cruel evil spirit,
Or the loving person
That God wants us all be?

The face in the mirror,
That we see everyday,
May not be fair and beautiful
Or perfect in every way.
But God made us all in His image,
And sees only our hearts,
When we kneel to pray.

If we had a magic mirror
That showed only what we want to see,
We would all be fair and handsome,
And no aging would there ever be.

But Alas!
There is no magic mirror
That can change the face we see.
So we must be content
To accept the face in the mirror
That God gave to you and me...

The Farmer

Up before dawn,
Gotta milk the cows
And feed the stock,
And with 14 hours of chores to do,
I can't slow down or stop.

Up before dawn,
Gotta fix the tractor
And mow the hay,
Then plow 20 acres
And shoe old Grey.

Up before dawn,
Gotta sharpen the ax
And chop some wood.
I'd sell this old farm
If only I could.

Up before dawn,
Gotta round up the hogs
And fix the boar.
Later, gotta do some trading
At the Country Store.

Up before dawn,
Gotta clear some new ground.
After planting the corn,
It's time for my Saturday bath,
Then take the family to town.

Up before dawn,
Gotta fix the leaky roof on the barn.
I'm behind on my mortgage,
And if I don't watch it,
I could lose the farm.

Up before dawn,
Gotta prune some fruit trees,
Then after cutting the wheat,
I'll rob the bees.

Up before dawn,
All this work is getting me down.
I'd like to sell off the farm
And move into town.

Moving into town sounds mighty fine,
But the wife and kids all said, "No!"
And started to cry.
Looks like I'll be farming this land
'Till the day that I die.

The Happy Hiker

It's spring time in the mountains,
And I'm here on the trail,
To hike where it leads me,
Across the wide green valleys
And up the high blue mountains
Beyond their misty veil.

There's sunshine over my shoulder
And a cool breeze on my face.
The blue skies make me smile
As I set a steady pace.

My steps are soft and easy;
There's no need to hurry,
No need to run a race.
I'm here to enjoy God's creation
In this serene and beautiful place.

There's a stream beside the trail,
And its music puts my mind at ease.
And the breeze plays a soft melody
As it caresses the flowers and trees.

There's a waterfall across the valley
With rainbows in the mist.
The rhododendrons are in full bloom--
Could heaven be more beautiful than this?

My worries and cares are all forgotten
As I view the scenes along the trail.
There's an eagle overhead,
And a mother deer and her fawn are
grazing in the vale.

As I near the mountain top and linger there to rest,
The view across the valley takes away my breath!
For the scene there before me,
As I look down from the crest,
Could only be painted by God,
As the mountains and the river turn to gold,
And the Sun sets in the west!

The Happy Hunter

I love to get out in the mountains
And go hunting in the Fall.
And each animal that I see,
I shoot and mount and hang'm
On my Trophy Wall.

Last week I bagged a mother deer and her fawn
That were grazing in the vale!
And yesterday, I shot a six-point buck
As I stalked him on the trail!

My trophies include big game
And other animals large and small.
And the thrill I get from shooting a deer
And her fawn or a bear and her cub
Makes me feel ten feet tall!

As a hunter, I am relentless;
Hunting seasons I ignore.
My pleasure counts the most;
I'm out to make a score!

Sometimes I bag a baby rabbit
Or A frisky little squirrel.
And I am not above shooting a baby bird--
It is a cruel world!

But there is something you should know
About my hunting style.
I'm not for bragging rights, notoriety or fame--
Because I only shoot the animals with my camera;
There is never any injure, blood or pain.

Then I take the pictures home
And hang them on my Trophy Wall.
Then I can enjoy beautiful animals all year long--
In Winter, Spring, Summer, and Fall.

The Hiker's Prayer

Hike with me, Lord,
This trail is long, rough, and steep.
My life is in your hands;
Hold me ever safely in your keep.

Thunder is echoing from the mountains,
And lightning strikes are drawing near.
But there is shelter from the storm
By your presence that calms my fear.

Sometimes the trail is slick and narrow,
And fallen trees and boulders block my way.
Keep my steps ever firm and sure,
Don't let me fall, Dear Lord, I pray.

Beautiful scenes are all around me,
And sometimes from the trail I stray.
But my indiscretions are all forgiven
When to you, Dear Lord, I pray.

Lord, This trail, at times, has been so lovely
With beautiful mountains, lakes and streams.
And the kindness and love of friends and family
Has made the trail a *hiker's dream*.

Now, Lord, I am feeling tired and weary
Because the trail has been so long.
Pain and sorrow have often been my companions,
But still my faith in you is ever strong.
Please give me strength to keep on hiking--
Until I reach your golden throne...

Joe Jr., Susan, Rosemary, Ginny

Little David, our youngest son

The Joy of Children

Their presence is like a beautiful sunrise
Shining into the chambers of my heart.

Their voices and laughter are like
The sound of music playing
Sweet melodies in my mind.

Their hugs and kisses are like a
Spring shower refreshing my spirit
And filling my heart with love.

Their goodbyes are like
The call of the mourning dove,
Beautiful, but sad and lonely...

The Life of a Man

If a man could live as long as a tree--
Maybe a thousand years or so,
Would he grow in wisdom, grace, and stature,
Or would he turn into a crabby old troll?

Would he embrace life as a peaceful river
And live each day like a beautiful dream?
Would he value life as a gift from God
And know its glory like a flowing stream?

Would he walk a path of honor and truth
And respect the rights of his fellowman?
Would he show the courage of a true brave heart,
And for justice and honesty take a stand?

Would he treat all people with due respect
Whether famous, rich, or poor?
Would he feed and clothe and cast no stones
To a destitute man standing at his door?

Would he be a true and loyal friend
And never judge or condemn his fellowmen?
Would he stand as bold as a great oak tree
And defend to the end his loyalty?

Would he face the storms of life
Without complaint to God or man?
Would be responsible for his own mistakes
And take the blame as best he can?

Would he be a loving husband and father
And work hard and long to ensure their care?
Would he always respect and honor his parents
And keep them ever in his prayer.

Would he measure up to the highest standard
Of a man with a compassionate and gentle soul?
Would he show kindness to all along the road of life,
Especially to the poor and very old?

But upon reflection,
How long a man lives may have no effect
on his character or soul.
It may be only what he chooses to be--
A man of refinement or a grouchy old troll.

The Little Church in the Valley

There's a little church in the valley,
Where fond memories beckon me,
Of family, friends and neighbors,
And how it used to be.

It was there we would gather
For church and Sunday School
And listen to the word of God
That rang so pure and true.

The old Pastor was a righteous man,
Who preached the old time faith--
Of Jesus and His love for all
And His saving grace.

And when the Spirit moved him,
Oh, how the old Pastor could preach!
And God would bless us everyone
As every heart was reached!

It was there we sang the old time hymns
Of love and praise that lift the hearts of men.
And as our voices raised on high,
It seemed the angels would join in.

Amen! Hallelujah! and Praise the Lord!
were often heard that made the Devil quake!
And "shouting in the spirit" by many of the saints
would make the old building shake!

As the Pastor closed each service,
He always gave an altar call,
And sinners convicted of their sins
To their knees would fall.

Then there were tears of joy!
Oh, how their faces would glow!
Because all was right between them
and the Lord,
As He welcomed them to the fold.

How quickly the years have passed
Since those precious bygone days
When we were all together
As we knelt there to pray.

The old Pastor and many of the congregation
have gone on to their reward.
Mom, Dad, three sisters and four brothers have left us too
And now are present with the Lord.

But we can still feel their love
And gentle spirits on those very special days
When we gather in the little church
And lift our hearts in praise.

*Dedicated to the Banner, Virginia
Assembly of God Church Congregation
of the late forties and early fifties.
God blessed us all--everyone!*

The Mountain of Life

We all must follow a lonely road
As we climb the Mountain of Life.
Sometimes the road is clear and easy,
Sometimes obscured by strife.

Many dangers abound on the Mountain;
Life is not always sunny and bright.
There may be storms of pain and illness;
Grief and despair can overtake us--
Turning the Mountain darker than night.

Many people we'll meet on the Mountain,
Some beautiful and loving,
Whose friendship will never fail.
While others are evil predators,
That seek only to divert us off the trail.

Millions are on the Mountain of Life,
And many have fallen along the way.
Burdened by the cares of the world,
They may have neglected to pray.

When it seems to go on is hopeless,
You're tired, depressed and lonely,
And the road is just too steep to climb.
Remember, God,
Friends and family are always near you;
They'll help you any time.

No matter how long or steep the road,
We must never give up the fight.
For when we reach the Mountain top,
Victory will be in sight!

The Old Country Store

I'd like to wander back to the Old Country Store,
And see it once again as it was before.
With shelves stocked from ceiling down to floor
With everything you'd ever want and more.

I'd greet the old timers as I walked through the door,
As they sit there playing checkers and arguing about the war,
Or maybe about the weather and what it holds in store.

In winter,
The old potbelly stove would be glowing cherry red,
And tobacco smoke would be thick
As it swirled around your head.
And old Grady would be chewing Brown Mule,
And spitting like a dunce that had never been to school.

If there was a nickel in my pocket,
It had to be a joke,
Because I grew up during the Great Depression,
And there wasn't any money to waste on
Jaw Breakers, Popsicles, Bubble Gum or Coke.

There were special smells in The Old Country Store:
Like leather goods, dry goods, bananas,
Bread, bologna, kerosene and at least a 100 more.
And if you went there hungry, it could spoil your whole day,
Because you'd buy so many things for which you couldn't pay.

Now, The Old Country Store has faded from the scene.
Replaced by Wal-Mart, K-Mart, and other big stores
That are so impersonal, they really are obscene.

But The Old Country Store had its day in the sun.
It served us all so well, but now its day is done.
I hated to see it go because it meant so much to me.
But it'll still be there, but only in my memory...

The Old Home Place

There's a deserted old house on a lonely hill,
Forlorn and neglected, it sits there still.
It once was a house of beauty and grace;
It was our home, The Old Home Place.

Its rooms once echoed with laughter and kids at play,
But now, there's only silence at the close of day.
Once there was light and activity in every room;
Now, there's only emptiness, shadows and gloom.

The old house holds memories of long ago...,
Of Mom and Dad and the family fold.
Those memories grow fonder each passing day...
Since Mom and Dad have passed away.

Each evening at supper time, Dad would pray,
And thank the Lord for His blessing that day.
And Mom would sing a beautiful refrain.
How I wish I could hear their voices again...

Many decades have passed since
those childhood years,
When life was sweet and full of cheer.
But I can still hear their laughter
And see the smiles on their face,
And remember again...
The wonderful times we shared
At the Old Home Place.

The Old House

There's an empty old house that sits on the hill--
Just waiting for someone its rooms to fill.
Abused and neglected, it sits there alone--
Just needing a family to make it their home.

Inside no laughter is heard with children at play;
No call for a family to supper at close of day.
No prayers are said or kind words are spoken.
The old house looks so lonely with a heart that is broken.

The doors are sagging; the steps are worn.
Some windows are broken; the curtains are torn.
Shingles are missing; the roof has a leak,
But what stories it could tell if only it could speak.

Then one day,
A young couple with children arrived on the scene--
Looking for a house to complete their dream.
They bought the old house and soon renovations were done.
Now, it is gleaming like new in the noon-day sun.

There are new shingles on the roof, new windows and doors;
New paint on the walls, new carpet on the floors,
Happy voices and laughter fill the rooms once more,
And the old house seems to be smiling from every window and door.

The Old Man's Poem of Secrets

He looked at least 100 years old
By the history written on his face.
The wrinkles, smiles and laugh lines
Spoke eloquently of a life's long race.

Bowed and stooped by age,
His steps were slow and paced,
But the sparkle in his eyes
Was something age had not erased.

I met him on the trail,
And we stopped to pass the time of day.
I engaged him in a conversation
To see what words of wisdom he would say.

He said, "Young man, (to me age 19)
I'm almost one hundred years old,
And I would like to pass on some secrets
To few other people I have told."

Then, with a far-away look in his eyes,
He began to tell me about his life.
He said, "Once I had a loving partner;
We were married for eighty years--
She was a wonderful wife."

Then he recited the following poem for me,
And I must say, I took it all to heart:

Treat Her Gentle

How fortunate is the man who finds a wife
To walk by his side all through life.
So, Treat her gentle with loving care,
And through good times and bad,
She will always be there.

She has class;
Treat her with respect.

She has grace;
Treat her with dignity.

She has beauty;
Treasure her as a pearl of great price.

She is the Mother of your children;
Rejoice at the beauty & miracle of birth.

She is your best friend;
Never take her for granted.

She is a great cook, homemaker, and Mother.
Compliment her skill and talents often.

Her words and actions leave no doubt
That you are the man of her dreams.
Encourage her fantasy with tender words,
Hugs and kisses, gifts and flowers.

She has tender emotions,
And her heart is easily broken.
Treat her gentle and never betray her love.

I then thanked the old man for his sage advice,
and we parted as friends.

As of December 22, this year,
my wife and I will have been married 67 years.

Lovely Miss Shirley Stallard, who became my darling wife

The Old Mill by the Stream

I can hear in my memory
And at night in my dreams
The sound of the old mill
As its wheel turns in the stream.

It was there I first met you
And looked on your face
And was enchanted forever
By your beauty and grace.

Deep was the mill pond,
As was the love in my heart,
And sweet was your promise,
That we'd never part.

Over sixty years later with a family I adore,
I love you still; I love you more.
The old mill is still there grinding out corn,
And our lives, like the old mill,
Has weathered many a storm.

Now, as I walk by the old mill
With you by my side,
My heart overflows with joy and pride.
How thankful I am, those many years ago,
I stopped by the old mill,
And you said, "Hello!"

The Old Oak Tree

The Old Oak Tree, that stands on the hill,
Has known lightning, wind and hail.
For over 400 years, it has defied them all
And continues to prevail.

From a tiny acorn into a mighty tree it grew,
With branches ever reaching to the sky.
Providing shelter for creatures of the forest
And shade for all passers-by.

Bushels of acorns on its branches grow,
To feed birds and animals through the winter cold.
And in Autumn, its leaves put on quite a show,
Before enriching the earth so other trees will grow.

If man was as unselfish as the Old Oak Tree,
And though less of self and more of his fellowman,
We'd all be taller in the eyes of God,
And this would be a more wonderful land.

A strong grape vine encircles the Old Oak Tree
In a loving embrace.
And like your love that encircles my heart,
No one could ever take your place.

I carved our initials on the Old Oak Tree
So many years ago.
And like our lives, it has weathered life's storms,
And still stronger grows.

And if we could live as long as the Old Oak Tree,
My love for you would still brighter glow.
For unlike the tree, true love never dies,
But only continues to grow.

The Optimist

The Optimist is a cheerful man;
To him the world is a beautiful place
Of sunshine, rainbows and waterfalls,
And a smile is always on his face.

In words and actions,
The Optimist conveys to all around,
There's more to life than death and gloom.
His smile and laughter is like the sunshine
That brightens up a room.

Whether in person or on the phone,
He'll lift your spirits high.
His first words will make you feel at ease,
And soon you'll be flying in the sky.

How can a person be so upbeat
In this world of pain and gloom?
I'd say it takes a very special person,
And I hope you'll meet one soon.

The Pain of Regret

If I could stop the spinning earth
And reverse the passage of time,
I would change the events of yesterday
To give me peace of mind.

Selfish actions would be reversed,
And all my mistakes would disappear.
Words of ridicule, spoken in haste,
No one would ever hear.

Bad decisions would be reversed.
Opportunities lost would be redeemed.
Honor and integrity would be the hallmark
Of every transaction that is seen.

Kindness and respect would be my motto.
Justice and fairness would be my creed.
My word would be a badge of honor
That I would wear with pride and esteem.

God and country would take priority
Over self-interest and dishonor, it brings.
Family and friends would always come first
With no time for frivolous and worthless things.

Wisdom and knowledge I would seek as treasure,
Understanding and judgment as silver and gold.
Food and clothing I would dispense with pleasure,
But my gifts of charity only God would know.

The poor and sick would see my compassion,
The grieving and old my sympathy and respect.
Gossip and hearsay would be abolished
For statements that are true and correct.

How often we fail to do what's right
When emotions and pride blind our sight.
Some mistakes can be fixed, for others, it's too late--
For these the pain of regret will be our fate.

The Prodigal Son

I was young and restless.
I longed to be on my own.
So, I left my Mom and Dad;
I left a loving home.

Soon I fell into bad company,
On drugs and alcohol I was stoned.
I thought I had found the good life;
But soon I found I was alone.

My inheritance was squandered;
My money was all gone.
Desperate, no job or income,
Now broke, homeless and alone.

For years, I wandered the back alleys and ghettos;
My youth and the good years wasted and gone.
In a store front window, I saw my reflection--
A young man, old before his time.
In dirty and threadbare clothes,
Unshaved, hair uncut, a homeless man
Wandering the streets alone.
What could I do? Where could I go?
Oh, how I long for home!

But would Mom and Dad still want me?
Would they welcome me back home?
My shame was more than I could bear.
I knew I had broken their hearts
When I left them there alone.

I fell on my knees and prayed
As the tears rolled down my face.
Lord, Please help me get home somehow.
I want to make it right with Mom and Dad.
I long to see them now.

How I got home, I'll never know,
But here I stand outside the door.
Mom and Dad are here to welcome me
With tears, smiles, and loving arms...

The River of Time

Time is like a river that is flowing quickly by,
And we're all adrift in the current,
That we can never stop or slow down...
No matter how we try.

Time is taking us all on a journey
Some to a life that is fulfilling and great.
But for others, it may be a tragic shipwreck,
When all hope is dashed on the rocks of fate.

The River of Time is full of dangerous rapids
That can rip our lives to shreds.
So, we must keep a constant lookout
For a clear channel up ahead.

If we could reverse The River of Time
And make its current flow back again,
We could start our lives all over,
And change the things that might have been.

But Alas!
The River of Time flows only forward,
And its current is swift and strong--
That leaves us only a fleeting moment
To do what's right or wrong.

As we drift with Time's swift current,
How quickly our journey seems to end,
And we're cast like useless flotsam
Upon some barren shore--quickly forgotten,
Except by family and our friends.

The Wanderer

Just over the next mountain,
A paradise I'll find
With honey in the comb
And grapes on the vine.

Just over the next mountain,
I'll find sweet content.
I'll forget the cares of the world
And the wasted life I have spent.

Just over the next mountain
No more lonely nights will I know.
Surrounded by Loveones,
I'll bask in love's glow.

Just over the next mountain,
All my dreams will come true.
I'll find again the warmth of your arms
And the love we once knew.

I've crossed over the mountain
To the valley below,
But doubts fill my thoughts
The closer I go.

Will she still want me,
Or is rejection my fate?
Will there be love in her eyes,
Or have I waited too late?

In an instant,
My doubts have all faded away.
She's here in my arms holding me near,
And the love in her eyes has banished all fear.

The Winter of 2015

Spawned in Siberia like a nightmare dream,
Pandora came out of the NW with a howl and a scream!
Artic blasts so cold that few had seen--
It was the mother of all storms in 2015!

Down over Alaska and Canada to the Lower 48,
Wave after wave of snow, ice and cold!
From Chicago to Boston and Nashville to Richmond,
The temperature kept dropping to zero and below!

One, two, three, four arctic blasts in a row!
No one was ready because we didn't know
That Pandora would be so long and bitterly cold.
From North to South, it was a knockout blow!

Snow and ice piled up in roadways and streets;
Cars, houses and barns were all covered in snow.
Many wrecks on the freeway--don't drive we are told!
A lot of cars in the ditch and the schools were all closed.

There were roofs caving in from ice and snow!
Water pipes were bursting from the bitter deep cold!
Families were snowbound and prisoners in their homes!
The National Guard assisted the stranded and alone!
The question in most minds was,
"Will this storm ever end? I want to leave home!"

Pandora brought a lot of pain, grief and disgust;
For years to come, I am sure it will be cussed.
But all were thankful if their loved ones were OK,
And were looking forward to sunshine and flowers
in April and May.

Folks and Strangers, I have always, since I was knee high to a Jack Rabbit, loved the West and everything about it. I have watched hundreds of western movies, read hundreds of western books and lived "where the wild west begun" in Fort Worth, Texas for over 20 years. I wanted to retire to Colorado, but got shot out of the saddle by a pretty little woman who wanted to head back East. Now, I still read westerns and watch western movies and visit out West as often as I can. I had fun branding the following lines on this page and I hope you enjoy reading them.

Things I like About the West

Spanish Missions and lost gold Mines
Bank loot hidden and hard to find

Mountain men and trapper lines
Beaver, Grizzly Bears, and Mountain Lions

Cliff Dwellers, rock castles and old Indian trails
Dried up waterholes and desert wells

Homesteaders, farmers, and wagon trains
Nesters, barbed wire fences and open range

Fence cutters, squatters and water holes
Mountain meadows that no one knows

Cowboys, Indians and outlaws
Rattle Snakes, lizards and things that crawl

Brahma Bulls and bucking horses at rodeos
Pretty girls and wild west shows

Boots and saddles, chaps and spurs
Range wars and feuds that go on for years.

Long Horn cattle and round up time
Quarter horses that can turn on a dime

Ten gallon hats and Levi jeans
Sour dough biscuits and Pinto beans

Mining shafts and stamping mills
Hard rock miners and steam jack drills

Gold nuggets, copper and silver ores
Black smith shops, livery stables ad general stores

Winchester rifles, fast draw artist and Colt 44s
Green Horns, long horse rides and saddle sores

Bonanzas, gold rushes and mining claims
Bank and train robberies by Jesse James

Tin Horn gamblers that lie and cheat
Followed by gun fights in the street

Old forts, Indian villages and trading posts
Wild boom towns that turned to ghosts

Cattle drives to Dodge and Abilene
River crossings and raging streams

Stage coaches and steam engine trains
Snow-capped mountains and endless plains

Sheriffs and Marshals of town-taming fame
Indian treaties broken and whose to blame

Big buckle belts, Spanish spurs and high heel boots
Cattle and horse thieves and other owl hoots

Sod houses, line cabins and old shacks
White-faced cattle, milk cows and big hay stacks

Buck boards, wagons and one horse hacks
Gun fights, fist fights and rifle racks

Hanging valleys and waterfalls
Ice caves, lava tubes and coyote calls

Antelope, burros and wild horses running free
Killers, outlaws and rustlers on a hanging tree

Texas Ranger on an outlaw's trail
To get his man will ride through hell

Partner, I could keep this up for another week,
But I guess by now, you are bored stiff or fast asleep.
So, if you want to add more, just be my guest.
As for me, I am going to take a rest. Adios, Partners ZZZZZZ

Thinking Young

Well, They say I'm getting old,
And in years, I'd have to agree.
But I can still climb the mountains,
And I can still jump and run.
'Cause you are just as old as you think,
And I am still thinking young.

Some people are still young at 93,
While others are already old at 21.
Getting old is really just a frame of mind.
'Cause you are just as old as you think,
So, keep on thinking young.

How old does a man get to be
Before he can have no fun?
Well, I still hike the trails
Where the streams and rivers run.
'Cause you are just as old as you think,
And I am still thinking young…

Sometimes I feel like a 100,
But I don't let feelings get in my way.
I am bound to do the things I love
Till they lower me into the grave.
'Cause you are just as old as you think,
And I am still thinking young.

Why deprive one's self of the pleasures
Of a life that can be joyful and free?
You can still do a whole lot of living
Before this life is done.
'Cause you are just as old as you think,
So, keep on thinking young.

Now, people can't live forever,
But they can all their lives think young.
So just do the things you love,
And keep on playing in the sun.
'Cause you are just as old as you think,
So, keep on thinking young.

Thorns

It seems that God made thorns
To stick and torment man
Because every time
We pick a Blackberry,
Thorns stick us in the hand.

And as we reach for that beautiful rose,
Its thorns will stick us too.
It may be that God wants to remind us
That things in life worthwhile
Are worth some pain to do.

Could it be that there's a cost
To win the race of life,
And thorns are just a reminder
That we all must pay the price?

Some people's character is full of thorns;
Social graces they have few.
They may be beautiful in appearance,
But their love is never true.
And if you get too close to them,
Their thorns will stick in you.

How I wish that God had put some thorns
On the apple tree.
Then maybe Adam and Eve
Wouldn't have eaten the forbidden fruit,
And put a curse on you and me.

Our Savior was crowned with thorns,
And mocked as King of the Jews.
Then they nailed him to a cross,
And on that cross, he died for me and you.

Three Score Years and Ten

God created man to live forever
In perfect peace with Him.
And He placed him in a beautiful garden
Free from evil and sin.
But evil entered the garden,
And man was tempted and sinned.
So, God reduced man's life span
To three score years and ten.

Since our life span has been shortened,
We must work quickly to accomplish all we can.
And no life is ever wasted
Spent in service to God and our fellow man.

If we live beyond God's promise
To 80 years or more,
We can expect only pain and sorrow
And heartache for loved ones gone before.
The "Golden Years" are really just a myth,
That so many would like to believe,
Because old age is nothing easy
When dealing with pain, loneliness and disease.

So soon our life's work is over,
And there is no reason to stay.
It'll be time to say our goodbyes
And to silently fly away.

I am grateful for the years that God has given,
But how wonderful our lives could have been
If only He had extended our years
To a million score years and ten.

Even though our life on earth has been shortened,
God, in His wisdom, conceived a plan
To restore our life eternal before the fall of man.
He sent His only Son to redeem us all again
That we may live forever in perfect peace with Him.

Tick-Tock, Tick-Tock

Tick-Tock, Tick-Tock
The clock ticks off the seconds of time.
How quickly the years go by.
And the older we get, time speeds up
And really begins to fly.

Tick-Tock, Tick-Tock
Leave not your life to fate.
Waste not your time, but set your goals;
Take charge before it's too late.

Tick-Tock, Tick-Tock
We will never pass this way again;
We have but one life to spend.
But how magical is that precious life--
To waste it would be a sin.

Tick-Tock, Tick-Tock
On the scale of time,
Our lives are infinitely small.
But each moment of time,
Opportunity cries out;
Be sure to answer her call.

Tick-Tock, Tick-Tock
There's a part for all on the stage of time;
Some parts are large and some are small.
But when the final curtain comes down,
God will decide if our part was played well---
He will make that call.

Tick-Tock, Tick-Tock
When will our journey end?
The Master Time Keeper decides the date;
So, always be ready my friend.

Time

Time, What is time?
A life lived,
Some heartache,
Some pain
Some sunshine,
Some rain
A spouse loved,
Children adored.
Friends made,
Loved ones enjoyed

Death

Death, What is death?
A brief interlude on our journey
To a more perfect world.

To Really Live

I want to go sailing down a crystal river
And feel it merge with its mother sea--
And climb to the peak of the highest mountain
And view the earth and its majesty.

I want to blast off into outer space
Past the Sun and the planets, we see--
And continue on to the edge of the universe
To find the end of eternity.

I want to set sail on a stormy ocean
And feel the power of the raging sea--
Then feel the fear that chill men's souls
Before God sets their spirits free.

I want to look into the eyes of a beautiful woman
And know her love is just for me--
Then witness the birth of our little baby
And marvel at the miracle and mystery.

I want to walk up heaven's streets of gold
Where angel's feet have trod--
And meet and shake hands with Christ, The Lord
And His Father, All Mighty God.

To really live, one must almost die
And challenge body and spirit to the nth degree--
And not be afraid to live life to the fullest--
To experience the fear and ecstasy...

Tree Swallows

Like thistledown in a breeze,
The Swallow soars the sky with ease.
Over meadows, hills and dell,
No bird can fly quite as well.

Flies with ease, soars with grace,
No bird can match it in a race.
Quick in flight, keen of eye,
Catches insects on the fly.

Soaring up, swooping down,
Barely inches from the ground.
Darting left, dodging right,
Aerobatic in its flight.

Feathers shimmer in the light,
Colors ever changing during flight.
Iridescent green, white and blue,
Like a sunbeam on the morning dew.

Could there be a life so free,
As to fly away on a gentle breeze,
Or to catch the wind as it passes by,
And let it lift you high in the sky--
To loiter there on feathered wings,
To gaze in wonder at God's creation of
Mountains, valleys, lakes and streams.

True Friends

True friends are hard to come by,
Their support and fidelity are rare.
When you find them, treasure them always;
Their friendship is beyond compare.

What is a true friend you may ask;
How can one tell if their friendship is true?
Is it the charming words they speak,
Or does it boil down to what they will do?

Many words could describe a true friend,
But loyalty, unselfishness, and honorable
would rank among the best:

Loyalty--Faithful, devoted and true,
Their support is never in question;
They will always stand by you--
No matter what others may do.

Unselfishness--Generous, charitable and giving,
Their friendship is never for gain.
If ever in need, they'll be there to help you
With no thought of credit or fame.

Honorable--Honest, fair, and sincere,
You can trust them to do the right thing.
Whether rich or poor, in good times and trouble,
They'll treat you just the same.

A true friend may be a loved one--a husband or wife;
Or a military buddy--a comrade during the horrors of war,
Or a neighbor across the street, who has helped you often,
But never keeps score.

A true friend will always lift you up;
He displays no jealousy, disrespect or greed.
His words are always complimentary and positive,
And his actions clearly show, he is a true friend indeed.

How could we live without friends;
Our lives are not lived alone.
We need the warmth and fellowship of others;
Our hearts are not made of stone.

Two Roads

There is a road that leads to heaven;
It is narrow and it's straight.
And there is a road that leads to hell;
It is wide and so easy to take.

But the road that leads to heaven
Is to eternal life they say.
But the road that leads to hell
Is where for all your sins you'll pay.

So, a decision must be made
By each one of us today---
Would you rather follow Christ
And live forever beyond the grave,
Or would you rather follow Satan
And forever be his slave?

Some people say there is no heaven,
While others say there is no hell.
And I must agree, it is all a matter of faith.
But if there is a heaven and a hell,
And you reject the Lord,
Then, Oh, what a terrible mistake!

Valley of the Lonesome Pine

There's a valley in the mountains
Where the lonesome pine tree grows.
And it is there my true love waits
Who I left so long ago.

It was our secret meeting place
Beneath the lonesome pine.
We would talk about our wedding plans
And the day she would be mine.

Then one day,
We argued about another suitor,
Who tried to steal her love from me.
And in anger,
I left her there to sail upon the sea.

For many years I wondered
Across the seven seas.
And though I tried to forget her,
My mind could not be free.
For my heart was ever longing
For the girl I left that day,
And with her I longed to be.

With an aching heart,
I returned to the mountains,
And swore I would never leave.
I'd marry my one true love,
And forever happy we would be.

Eagerly, I searched the faces as
I stepped down from the train,
But her loving face I did not see.
I asked old friends about her,
But in silence, they turned away.
Then an old man whispered softly,
"She waits beneath the lonesome pine;
You'll find her there today."

With a joyful heart,
I rushed to meet her beneath
the lonesome pine.
But there I saw only a cold grave stone
engraved with cryptic lines--
Words that forever tore my world apart!
For on the stone was my Darling's name,
Date of birth, death and the words:
She died of a broken heart.

Walk with Me, Lord

Walk with me, Lord;
I can't make this journey alone.
There is danger all around me,
And I am a long way from home.

Walk with me, Lord;
Pitfalls of evil are ever near me,
And sometimes my faith gets low.
Give me strength to fight temptation;
Don't let me lose my soul.

Walk with me, Lord;
This life is filled with pain and sorrow,
And it's so hard to understand.
But we know there will be a bright tomorrow
When we reach the promised land.

Walk with me, Lord;
Guide me ever in the way I go.
Teach me love and understanding
As your nail-scared hand I hold.

Walk with me, Lord--
Through the valleys of temptation
And across the mountains of doubt and fear.
Let me never doubt or falter
When my journey's end is near.

Wanderlust

Here's to the roads I long to travel,
And to the lands I long to see.
And here's to the wanderlust in my soul
That will never let me be.

Here's to the mountains I long to climb,
And to the seas I long to cross.
And here's to the woman I'll always love
And to the dreams forever lost.

Here's to the home I'll never have
And to a family and to friends.
And here's to all the things that I will miss,
And to all the things that could have been.

Here's to arms I long to hold me
And to the lips I long to kiss.
And here's to the one I'll ever long for,
And to the one I'll ever miss.

Beauty, Peace and Majesty

Waterfalls

When my troubles overwhelm me,
And it's peace my mind is in need,
Then to a waterfall I am going
Where my worries are relieved.

How soothing the sound of a waterfall
As it tumbles into the stream.
How beautiful the misty rainbows
As sunshine floods the peaceful scene.

In a world of pain and sorrow,
How depressing our lives can be,
But waterfalls are a gift from heaven--
To inspire and set us free.

There's something magical about a waterfall
That awakens a sense of wonder
And moves many to write songs and poems,
Or to start their lives anew--
All because they saw a waterfall,
And were inspired by the view.

No words can truly describe a waterfall,
And no scene can ever compare
To its beauty, peace and majesty--
Could it be God's presence there?

Since the dawn of creation,
Waterfalls have been flowing,
And may God ever let them flow--
For the joy and peace of mankind
In this troubled world here below.

What Are You

A deadbeat or a worker?
A helper or a shirker?
A planner or a bungler?
A steady hand or a fumbler?
A giver or a taker?
A lover or a hater?
A frugal person or a wasteful spender?
An encourager or a dissenter?
A winner or a loser?
A teetotaler or a boozer?
A supporter or a critic?
A believer or a cynic?
A follower or a leader?
A loyal person or a cheater?
A fighter or a quitter?
A straight talker or a deceiver?
An honest person or a liar?
A believer or a denier?
A promoter or a mocker?
An achiever or just a talker?
A Christian or a sinner?
A true friend or a pretender?
A wise person or a wiseacre?
A sympathetic person or a faker?
A peacemaker or a hazer?
A responsible person or a hell raiser?

Unless we practice self-deception,
In our hearts we know for certain
That none of us measure up completely
To the ideal and perfect person.
But we should strive each day
To amend our errant ways,
And look to Christ as our example
Of a life that was perfect in every way.

Wisdom of Years

Give me, Oh Time, your wisdom of years
That I may wisely say and do
Those things that will be a blessing to others
In this world as I'm passing through.

Give me, Dear Mother, a touch of your kindness
That God in his wisdom bestowed.
A love for your children unfathomable,
And a heart filled with love and compassion--
More precious than diamonds or gold.

Give me, Dear Father, your strength of character
That I may be honest, responsible and bold.
The type of person all people will honor
In this life wherever I go.

Give me, Dear Friends, of your loyalty--
The kind that lasts down through the years,
And a friendship that is giving and caring
That will see me through heartaches and tears.

Give me, Dear Lord, the gift of your love
That will forever dwell deep in my soul
That I may be kind and loving to all--
Never cruel, selfish or cold.

These gifts are rare and precious
And can never be purchased or sold.
Blessed are all who receive them;
Their value can never be told.

Woman

Graceful in movement,
Kind and gentle in manner,
Fair and lovely in appearance,
Always compassionate and loving--
The envy of Angels.

Lovely eyes, hair and face,
Soft, creamy skin with a beautiful glow,
Blessed with a rare enter beauty--
God's most lovely creation.

Loving arms to hold you,
Tender lips to kiss you,
Soft hands to caress you,
Beautiful eyes to adore you,
Warm, pleasing voice to call your name--
Fortunate is the man who wins her love.

Patient, kind and gentle as a Mother,
Whose love is more sure than a sunrise,
And more eternal than the universe.
In her heart,
There is only love and affection for her children
Even though they may stray from her guidance
many times. God blessed woman, our Mothers,
With all the beauty, love, kindness and saintly qualities
That it is possible for the human spirit to possess.

Woman—A Man can never feel content or complete
without her presence in his life.

Words

Our words
Project an image of the contents of our heart,
Whether it be hate or malice,
Love or kindness that our words impart.

Words of love,
How sweet the sound,
When spoken by someone dear,
Like music to our longing ear.

Words can heal a broken heart,
And comfort love ones when they part.
Can draw us near at close of day,
And bring peace and solace when we pray.

Words can inspire and motivate,
Win our love or make us hate.
Can drive us forward to do our best,
And help us endure life's toughest test.

Words of kindness
Can left us up when we are down,
Produce a smile, erase a frown.
Can drive to flight the darkest night,
And help us embrace God's love and light.

Words of hope will light the way
For someone who has gone astray.
Can lead them to a better life,
Free from fear, hate and strife.

Words of blessing,
Came from Christ the Lord,
Proclaiming to all God's rich reward.
Eternal life, could we ask more...
Peace and joy on heaven's shore.

World of Death and Sorrow

This old world is grieving, weeping
From the pain that we all know,
And from the loss of Dearest love ones
That break our hearts and grieve us so.

From disease, accident, war and murder,
There are so many ways to go.
And death has no respect of persons;
It greedily takes the young and old.

Each generation lives only briefly
As they quickly pass from young to old.
Then grieving love ones gather round them
As they say goodbye and go.

But the pain our hearts are bearing,
No one can ever know--
Unless they've lost a Dearest love one--
Taken from the family fold.

Is there no end to all the suffering
We must endure down here below?
Where is God when death comes calling--
Does He take no notice of death's evil toll?
Or does He bow His head in sorrow
And feel the pain that we all know?

But there is hope beyond this veil of tears,
Christ paid the price a long time ago.
Someday we'll be reunited with our love ones,
And we will never let them go...

You've Got to Laugh

Sometimes this life don't seem worth living;
There's too much taking and not much giving.
Sometimes the pain is hard to bear,
And the sorrow so deep that we can't share.
The heartache and grief make life so trying;
You've got to laugh to keep from crying.

Trouble and conflicts are all around.
The world is in chaos; no rest is found.
There is talk of peace, but they just keep lying;
You've got to laugh to keep from crying.

People out of work; no money coming in.
It's a constant struggle for families and friends.
COVID and Democrats got the Country shutdown.
It's a time for giving and a time for sharing;
You've got to laugh to keep from crying.

I forgot my mask; they won't let me in the store.
The baby is hungry and needs milk for sure.
It's ten miles back to the house--
COVID restrictions can be so trying;
You've got to laugh to keep from crying.

Many of our kids are on alcohol and drugs.
The Country is overrun with rioters, illegals and thugs.
Biden, A socialist is running for president,
But for months he has been in his basement hiding--
How could anyone in him be confiding;
You've got to laugh to keep from crying.

Your spouse is unfaithful
And has found someone new.
She's been cheating for years,
But you never knew.
There is an ache in your heart
There is no denying;
You've got to laugh to keep from crying.

You can't get on Facebook; you can't connect!
Your iPhone is dead--Oh, what the heck!
You got pictures to post and sites to share,
And things to see, and Face Book ain't fair.
Messages are piling up, but there is no replying;
You've got to laugh to keep from crying.

Democrats keep saying they'll bring prosperity to all;
Just give me your vote is their constant call.
But it's "pie in the sky" some fools are buying;
You've got to laugh to keep from crying.

For thousands of years, men have fought and died
For land, religion, glory, and pride.
Will they ever end the slaughter, and dying?...
You've got to laugh to keep from crying.

There's illness and suffering on every hand,
And the angel of death prowls the land.
There's no victory in sight, but we must keep trying;
You've got to laugh to keep from crying.

www.ingramcontent.com/pod-product-compliance
Lightning Source LLC
Chambersburg PA
CBHW051431290426
44109CB00016B/1514